The **RISK** Paradox

www.amplifypublishing.com

The Risk Paradox: Life Lessons from 102 Amazing Risk-Takers

For more information, please contact:
Amplify Publishing, an imprint of Amplify Publishing Group
620 Herndon Parkway, Suite 320
Herndon, VA 20170
info@amplifypublishing.com

Library of Congress Control Number: 2021920951
CPSIA Code: PRV0622A
ISBN-13: 978-1-63755-153-0

Printed in the United States

For those seeking courage
to become themselves.

The
RISK
Paradox

Life Lessons from **102** Amazing Risk-Takers

Alan Ying & Doug Schneider

amplify

CONTENTS

INTRODUCTION

Doug Schneider met Alan Ying at a long-ago forgotten corporate event that took place sometime in 2006. They were both working at a large healthcare analytics company that pioneered the use of "big data" in healthcare—and that was just about the only thing they had in common. Doug was a corporate lifer in his second stint with the company, with ten years' cumulative experience in a business he loved. Alan had just sold his five-year-old healthcare software company to this big business and was trying to understand why anyone would be a corporate lifer. Doug was an introvert by nature who talked to one or two people at a corporate event, then headed out before the wine began to flow. Alan had been with the company for three days, and he had already met all fifty people at the event, many of whom Doug didn't know after working there for ten years. Alan was a doctor, and Doug took extreme measures to avoid the sight of blood.

Yet, as Alan shared his story, Doug became more curious about him . . . in a somewhat anthropological sense. Alan told Doug he was a doctor, but not a practicing one. It turned out that he'd left the cardiothoracic surgery program at Duke University on December 31, 2000. Motivated by a compelling vision of enabling busy doctors to access patient records on mobile devices, the next day he had no paycheck and was running a software company with no customers and several employees stuffed into a one-bedroom apartment. His wife was supporting them on a bare-bones medical resident salary, and collectively they had a few hundred thousand dollars of student debt. In April 2001, the business, Mercury MD, landed its first customer.

As Alan told the rest of the story—about raising capital from aunts and uncles (not his), landing customers, reading every book on leadership he could get his hands on once it dawned on him that he was *actually* running a company, and eventually selling the business at a good price—Doug didn't retain much. His mind was still stuck on some basic questions.

Who in their right mind would leave a residency in Duke's cardiothoracic surgery program to start a healthcare tech company?

Did this guy really raise his first major round of capital in the middle of the dot-com crash of 2001?

What possessed him to think he could land his software company inside of this conservative big business?

And, above all, why would someone choose, of their own free will, to attempt such things?

One thing on Doug's short list of strengths is tolerance for unusual people. And, at least inside the walls of this company, Alan was an unusual person. As Alan settled into his new role of chief medical officer, he asked Doug countless questions about product innovation, which was one of Doug's responsibilities. Even though Doug was a busy corporate, middle-management guy, he took the time to answer the questions as well as he could. They were good questions, but more than that, Doug grew curious about Alan's insatiable curiosity. He liked Alan, but he was still trying to figure him out.

It was clear from the moment Alan and Doug met that they viewed risk differently. While Alan was dropping out of Duke in his late twenties, Doug was haunted by an ambiguous relationship with risk. Doug loved the *idea* of entrepreneurship and innovation, but he struggled to figure out how to practice risk-taking in his own life. Doug had bounced between small and large tech companies for twenty years. It wasn't that he never took any risks; he had worked in plenty of small tech companies that were fraught with financial challenges. One of them even missed payroll, which is a memorable and definitive end to a risk-taking experience if ever there is one.

However, by the time Doug met Alan, he was quite comfortable being a risk-taker inside his corporate walls, where all failure was relative, and a paycheck every two weeks was a sure thing. It would take him another five years from the day they met to work up the courage to genuinely jump off a cliff at age fifty-five.

The more Doug got to know Alan, the more he realized that for all of their differences, they did have one thing in common: they were both fascinated by what motivates people to decide whether or not to take a risk and by how risk-takers deal with the obstacles they inevitably encounter—emotionally, rationally, and even physically. The more they discussed this, the more fascinated they became.

It's taken Doug and Alan the better part of fourteen years since they first met at that long-forgotten event to find the time and space to research and document their findings, but they never stopped asking each other questions. And it's the questions that won't go

vay that drive people to do seemingly crazy and inadvisable
things, like, for example, writing this book.

What This Book Is About

When we started this book, we had a sense that risk-taking was an
important topic—in our own lives and in the lives of many people—
and we had a massive curiosity about how accomplished people
deal with risk. We interviewed 102 people, and we quickly learned
that successful risk-takers embody the full diversity of the human
race. We talked to introverts and extroverts, men and women,
people who grew up poor and rich, immigrants and natives, and
risk-takers in their thirties, forties, fifties, sixties, and seventies. We
diligently captured the backgrounds, personalities, geographies,
motivations, and circumstances of risk-takers. For a long time,
no pattern emerged, and the secret sauce of risk-taking remained
elusive. Being analytic types, we persevered, figuring that more
data points were better than fewer.

To be sure, the stories we listened to were interesting. We heard
from someone who grew up rich but decided to pursue his passion
and raise his family in the inner city. Several people acquired
wisdom early in life the hard way, by transcending abusive child-
hoods. The premature death of a parent or close relative changed
the trajectory of several lives irrevocably. For some, the biggest risk
they ever took was figuring out how to create their own life outside
of a family business. Seemingly impulsive life decisions to quit a
job, move across the country, travel the world, or start a business
with no capital sometimes paid off in stunning ways. We learned
that people with nothing to lose can be astoundingly resilient.

But what were the patterns? How could we make sense—from

this smorgasbord of human behavior and circumstance—of risk-taking and risk-takers? About halfway through our interviews, we realized the first lesson was right in front of us. The people we were talking to were *alive*. They were deeply engaged in the world, in their lives. When they succeeded, they savored their accomplishment, and then they moved on to the next risk. When they failed, they took the lessons of those failures, often added a dose of humorous self-reflection, and searched for the next challenge.

Their stories embodied our first realization about risk-taking: Taking risks, even conventionally inadvisable risks, is necessary to fulfill our potential. Risk-taking often enriches lives, even when it doesn't enrich our bank accounts.

We also observed many people whose bank accounts were secure enough but kept taking risks. We wondered why.

In time, we came to understand that taking risk, in some significant way, is fundamental to becoming yourself. And becoming yourself, realizing your potential as a human being, is crucial to life fulfillment.

Risk-takers, sometimes consciously and sometimes with minimal introspection, are on a constant journey to realize their potential as human beings.

This finally led us to the Risk Paradox, which is this: taking a risk is the least risky thing that you can do to live a fulfilling life.

The Risk Paradox plays out time and time again in the stories that follow.

If you are searching for a formula for successful risk-taking, which is another way of saying a formula for life success, this isn't the book for you. Risk-taking is complicated, and we wouldn't be so presumptive as to offer one up.

But, if you believe—as we do—that risk-taking is essential to fulfilling your potential, then you can learn a lot from the people you are about to meet. One of their journeys, one of their motivations, just might remind you of yourself. And, perhaps, change your life.

Methodology

We began with the question of what motivates anyone to take a risk, especially with the possibility of both significant gain or significant loss. Why do some people head straight for the tornado while others run for cover at the first report of storm clouds?

Alan decided that we needed to interview one hundred people who had clearly taken some form of "inadvisable risk" by conventional standards. Doug thought twenty-five was a more reasonable number. We compromised on one hundred. We decided that Alan would do the interviews and Doug would do the writing.

We aimed for as much diversity we could find, in age, gender, and life background, and with enough life experience to be able to reflect on what they had done and why. We were interested from the beginning in how one's life stage affects their orientation toward risk. We also asked everyone whether they were shaped by nature ("I was born this way.") versus nurture ("Upbringing and life experience made me.").

By the time we finished our interviews, we had a more diverse and interesting set of risk-takers than we could have ever imagined. We ended up with a fifty-fifty split of men and women. Most of our interviewees were in their forties, fifties, or sixties, but we talked to seven people in their thirties and six who were seventy or older. Half of our risk-takers experienced a significant life crisis. A third of them took huge financial risks that an objective observer might call inadvisable. One in four divorced at some point, and nearly one in four had significant conflict with one or both of their parents that shaped the trajectory of their life. Twelve grew up poor, twenty-four grew up wealthy, and the other sixty-four were broadly middle class. Eleven suffered a life-altering personal health crisis.

In a few of the stories we have used pseudonyms where the life circumstances are particularly sensitive. In most cases, we have used actual names with permission from the interview subject.

Risk-taking, unlike medical research, does not occur inside of double-blind clinical trials. It occurs in the context of messy and chaotic human lives. Nevertheless, we've made efforts to connect our findings to external research on human motivation and decision-making, where applicable.

While performance reviews and critical feedback have their place, we believe all of us learn more from stories. We've met many fascinating, inspiring, incredible people on this journey. We're excited to share their stories with you.

Doug Schneider and Alan Ying
August 2021

CHAPTER ONE

The Practice of Risk-Taking

The simplest way to understand the practice of risk-taking is to start with a story.

Early on in our research, we met Alton Butler. Alton's life has all the risk-taking twists and turns that you could possibly envision. Alton is the living embodiment of the Risk Paradox.

There's no way Alton Butler should have made it.

The only son of a womanizing, abusive father and an abused mother, he grew up dirt poor on food stamps in rural Alabama. Alton's father was a truck driver. Alton slept in the same bed as his two older sisters.

"When I was nine years old, my dad stabbed my mom while we were sleeping in the next room. We heard the screaming and ran in to find Dad standing over Mom with a big hunting knife. I jumped across my mom to protect her, worried she was going to die. My dad was in a dire state. My older sister hit him, jarring the sense back into him, and he realized what he was doing. My mom was seriously hurt, but she ended up surviving."

Alton's parents split up, then got back together, saying it was "for the kids," even though Alton and his sisters knew it couldn't possibly be good for anyone in the family. The marriage broke apart for good a year later.

By the time his mom married his stepfather, his older sisters were out of the house. Alton says his stepfather is "a man who was never hugged by anyone." He was the bouncer at a local bar.

"When I was in the eleventh grade, I got home and saw my mom with a black-eye, and we got into a huge argument. Back then, I was a little wiry guy, but getting bigger. I tried to get my stepfather outside . . . I ended up telling my mom, 'Listen, I can't do this. I'm going to move out.' I was going into my senior year of high school. She said, 'No, I'll divorce him.' I said, 'Look, don't do that. I've already got a scholarship. I'm going away to college. And then I'm never looking back, so don't do that for me.' I ended up moving out, living on a guy's couch during my senior year. After that, I went away to college and played football."

Playing football was Alton's only ticket out of rural Alabama. His only scholarship offer was to play defensive back for a junior college, but that was good enough. He made it from the junior college to Jacksonville State University where he was a starter. After college, he even got a tryout with the Atlanta Falcons, but unfortunately, he lacerated his kidney, ending his pro football career.

Football got Alton out of rural Alabama, and he was definitely not going back. He picked up an unconventional side job in college. There was a dance club in Birmingham back then called Gippers that was—technically speaking—a male strip club. Alton loved to dance, and one night he won $1,500 in a dancing contest at Gippers—a lot of money for a twenty-two-year-old jobless athlete.

Alton started his own dance company traveling to the major tourist haunts of the South: Myrtle Beach, Panama City, and even up to Canada. For a few years Alton had a house in Panama City Beach where he and his team danced four nights a week at a club every summer. The money was good and the female company was easy to find, but Alton knew that dancing couldn't—or shouldn't—last.

Alton faced a Moment of Truth when he realized his dancing career needed to be over. He was listening to audio tapes over and over from the motivational guru Tony Robbins. Alton decided to take a shot at making it as an actor. As he says, "I loved to act and loved the limelight and, obviously, I'm not a shy guy at all."

This was enough of a plan. In his mid-twenties and desperately not wanting to go back home, Alton rented out his house in Panama City, left his girlfriend behind, packed his car, and drove to Hollywood with his dog and his best friend and enrolled in acting school.

Alton paid his way through acting school, found an agent, and got several acting jobs. Acting was paying the bills but was hardly steady work. Alton discovered that he hated auditioning. It was rarely about talent; more often it was about how you looked, and it was too political to be anything he'd want to do for the long term. Plus, Alton realized that he was a bit of a control freak, and as an actor he never really had control of his destiny.

Then Alton caught a few of the kind of breaks that . . . well . . . they make movies about. One day, a guy on the set asked Alton to join his flag football team. Flag football is a big deal in LA, and the guy knew that Alton used to play football for real. In exchange, the guy agreed to let Alton work behind the camera. Alton realized that working behind the camera was steadier work than working in front of it, and he was looking for steady work.

During filming breaks, Alton hung out with the young production managers using stage equipment, such as folding chairs, tables, and the tents covering the shoots. He noticed the equipment was often in bad shape, and the production managers—who were mostly women—were being treated shabbily by the equipment suppliers.

"I was friendly and started doing due diligence—asking how much they paid for this gear, who they got it from. I researched that company, then I went to the guy I was working with and asked, 'Why don't we put in fifteen hundred bucks each and buy this stuff? I'll talk the production coordinators into giving us a shot to rent it. I'll store the equipment at my house,'" Alton recounted.

"I asked the production managers, 'Listen, if I had my own gear, would you give me a chance? If you don't like it, you never have to pay me a dollar, and I'll never mention it again. Right now, you're getting this beat-up shit from this company, and they couldn't care less about you.' They gave me a chance. I ended up getting a job from one production team, and then I got another one, then I got another one. It just exploded."

A few years later, Alton's equipment rental business had eliminated its major competitor. Alton even hired some of their former managers to work for him. He gave up on his acting career, realizing he was never going to be George Clooney anyway. With the equipment rental business, he was in charge—whereas acting jobs were subject to the whims of directors.

Around this time, Alton noticed an attractive Armenian woman who worked at his local bank. For some reason, she was always the one who helped him when he went through the drive-through window. Then he ran into her at the health club, and they started dating. Being from rural Alabama and all, Alton thought Armenia was a city in northern California rather than a country in western Asia. Today, that woman is his wife of nineteen years, and they have two teenage children.

In keeping with the Risk Paradox, Alton didn't stop when he achieved success with his equipment rental business. He just kept taking risks. He moved his equipment rental business right in the middle of the Hollywood media district. Next door was a beat-up old building—Hollywood National Soundstage. Alton started hanging out with the owner, Dick, and he asked about buying the property. One day, Dick told him he was tired of the movie business and wanted out. He asked Alton if he wanted to buy the soundstage.

Alton made calls to the producers; he was researching how much business he could generate. The producers were willing to give a shot to the nice guy from Alabama. Alton didn't initially have the money to buy the soundstage, so he leased it from Dick for $40,000 per month. Eventually, Alton convinced the banks to give him credit for the building improvements he made as a down payment on a mortgage, making his monthly payments much less than the $40,000 lease.

Alton worked hard to rent out the soundstage, and he had figured out that the most reliable production money was in filming commercials rather than movies. Eventually, three out of every four commercials shot for TV in Hollywood were shot on his soundstage. When Apple shoots a commercial, they rent out the entire facility.

In less than ten years, Alton's equipment and soundstage rental business became a major player in Hollywood. He still has his deep Southern accent and—especially when he can't remember something he feels he should—he regularly refers to himself as a redneck. At the beginning of our interview, Alton warned us that he can talk until the moon comes down, but the more he talks, the more delightful the conversation becomes. It's easy to understand how Alton wins people over.

Alton kept taking risks. Next, he bought a ten-acre piece of land in Burbank, where almost no commercially zoned land is available, and he decided to open the first new soundstage in Hollywood in fifteen years—a 240,000-square-foot facility. The property wasn't zoned for commercial use, but that didn't stop Alton. He spent three years getting sued by residents, but he ultimately worked with the city to change the zoning laws. He sold some of his other properties to finance the deal.

We finally asked Alton about all the risks he took.

"To be honest with you, I never saw any of those decisions as risky, because I felt like they were calculated. Now looking back . . . Holy shit, yes, those were *huge* risks. But at the time, you don't look at it like that because that gives you an opportunity to fail. I only had one way out. Rappers rap to get out of the hood. In rural areas, country boys play ball to get out of the country. We've got no other opportunity."

We thought we are done talking with Alton about risk (*What else could there be to talk about?*) when Alton called us back. What he had to say was a fascinating insight into another form of risk altogether. One about relationships, not money.

Alton decided to reconnect with his father. Yes, the guy who stabbed his mother when Alton was nine years old. It wasn't that he excused his father's actions. He wanted to understand what happened, to heal wounds buried deep in his psyche. It was about forgiveness.

Reconnecting with his father wasn't simple or straightforward.

At first, he bought a house back in Alabama where he moved his father in with his uncle. Then the uncle committed suicide. So, Alton did what might be unthinkable to anyone who knew his life story: he moved his father out to Los Angeles. He moved the parent who caused him so much pain practically into his own backyard.

What Alton learned in the process about his own father's upbringing, and about his paternal grandfather, stunned him.

"I wanted to dig down to find out why my dad did what he did. I didn't want to live with this hate. So, I went back home. When I did, I found out about the way my dad was treated, and I was heartbroken. His own dad, who died before I was born, was the biggest piece of shit ever," he explained.

"They did not have electricity until my dad was sixteen. They didn't have running water. He didn't have a pair of shoes. I don't think he even knows when he quit school. My dad had to plow the fields with a mule named Doc, and that mule was his best friend," he said.

"My granddad made my dad sleep in the barn. He would beat my dad with a hot poker when he got to be nine or ten. My grandfather even tried to trade my dad for another mule. He tried to trade a human being for an animal. Mentally, what does that do to you?" he asked.

"Today, my dad is the gentlest and kindest person you could be around. We have made our peace."

CHAPTER TWO

Living with Risk

Most of us don't start out life in circumstances nearly as difficult as Alton's, but we can learn something from how he made decisions in the crucial moments of his life. All of us have good days, boring days, and days when things aren't going so well. If you think someone you know has a perfect life, it simply means you don't know them as well as you think you do.

All of us face Moments of Truth in our own lives; forks in the road where we must choose risk or more near-term certainty.

Risk is commonly defined as the potential for uncontrolled loss of something of value, or the intentional interaction with uncertainty. We think of it as the near-certain odds of significant change from current conditions, with uncertainty as to whether the change will be better or worse, or in what magnitude. It's the risky decisions where we choose between paths that make the difference in our lives.

Moments of Truth come in many different forms: getting fired or laid off, quitting a job because you can't take it anymore, the death of a close relative, or even reading a book that transforms your understanding of the world. We don't get to choose when these Moments of Truth occur. It's not the event itself, but how we respond emotionally and cognitively that matters.

Alton faced his first Moment of Truth when he saw his father abusing his mother; even at age nine, he realized that he needed to find a way out of an abusive, impoverished childhood. When his way out—playing football—was demolished by a lacerated kidney, he became a dancer. After dancing played itself out, he bet on himself by heading for Hollywood. At every Moment of Truth, consciously or unconsciously, Alton chose more risk over less risk.

***

Alan faced a Moment of Truth when he dropped out of the Duke cardiothoracic surgery program to start a healthcare tech company. He finally hit the point where he couldn't simultaneously complete the Duke program and launch a software company. Alan remembers the moment of decision like it was yesterday:

"My wife was also in residency, and she saw me working on this start-up and was supportive, saying, 'Look, we can handle anything together.' One night she said, 'I don't think I can adjust as fast as you, so I need some notice if we go off our medical path.' I asked, 'How much notice?' She said, 'Six months.' After this conversation, sometime in the spring, it was 2:00 a.m. I woke her up and said, 'Hey listen, I'm spending so much time on this start-up, I don't know why but I can't stop. That has to mean something. If it gets down to choosing between the company and surgery, there's a possibility that I quit the surgery program.' Which was absurd because I had just been named the intern of the year, and it's the best program in the country."

"I remember it was October, we still didn't have any customers. I had programmers working out of an apartment. We didn't have a fully functioning product yet. I had this conversation with myself. *Look, if I am eighty years old and I'm a world-renowned cardiothoracic surgeon, and I didn't give this a try, would I regret it?* And I answered *Yes.* And then I took the other side and I thought, *If I did this and I quit surgery and the company fails miserably, would I regret it?* and I thought, *No.* It was a five-minute conversation with myself. And then the next day, I went and talked with my program director and told him I was going to leave mid-year, which was a huge deal. To my program director's eternal credit, he was supportive and engineered a mid-year exit for me."

Livewiths

Risk doesn't occur in a petri dish, but rather in the chaos of a human life, so there is no empirically validated theory of risk-taking. Yet, in the lives of those we interviewed, we can identify some patterns of risk-taking and risk-takers.

We couldn't quite decide what to call these patterns. We tried *rules*, but rules imply a rigidity inconsistent with the behaviors we were observing. We thought about *guidelines*, but, for most people—and especially those who don't like rules—guidelines are things you can take or leave.

Doug remembered a course he took in the Stanford MBA program called Creativity in Business taught by Michael Ray. It was a fascinating exploration of creativity and a way to avoid more accounting and finance courses. His professor had each student keep a journal, focusing on one idea a week to make them better at creative thinking. Students had to "live with" these ideas all week. He made up a word and called them *Livewiths*.

The Creativity Livewiths changed every week. One was *Destroy Judgment, Create Curiosity*. Another was *Be Ordinary*. Doug's favorite, which certainly applies to risk-taking, was *Ask Yourself If It's a Yes or No*.

Many of the Livewiths were counterintuitive but seemed to work when applied to real life. The more deeply one reflected on and aligned behavior with the Livewith, the better one got at creativity—which was the whole point of the course.

We realized we were uncovering Livewiths in our interviews. A Risk Livewith is a way of thinking that guides decision-making about risk on a conscious or subconscious level. Livewiths are based on the lived experiences of others who have gone before you. Applying these Livewiths help clarify thoughts and decisions in the Moments of Truth that really make a difference.

Livewith One: The Risk Paradox

We've already introduced Livewith One: The Risk Paradox, that the least risky thing you can do with your life is to take risk. People who have nothing to lose, like Alton, vividly illustrate the Risk Paradox. We also found from our interviews that generating enough money to "not have to worry about money again" is a trap. Getting rich can lead to its own form of risk—that life loses meaning and purpose.

Most risk-takers understand the Risk Paradox deep in their bones. Taking risks, even when you don't get the results you want, has a way of leading to more choices and opportunities. But when you don't take risks at all, you often end up living out someone else's story—or a life dictated by circumstance—rather than living your own story.

Which is the riskiest thing of all.

Livewith Two: Head and Heart

Risk would be an easier topic if it were just about mathematical odds of something working out. While odds are part of any risk calculation, it's clear that people don't make decisions solely based on probabilities. A range of experiences and emotions factor into any decision. This is supported by our interviews and also by researchers who have identified that the brain's "limbic system ties both emotion and experience into your decisions."[1]

Alton didn't make any mathematical calculation to chuck his life in Florida and move to Hollywood. He had a hunch that he could find a way to make it there.

Traditional economics assumes that, armed with complete information, individuals act rationally. Given life's messiness, traditional economics has precious little to say about risk-taking.

In contrast, the emerging field of behavioral economics concerns itself with the limits, or boundaries, of rational actions and perfect information. Behavioral economists emphasize heuristics, which they define as a hands-on, trial-and-error, iterative approach to learning. They estimate that humans make 95 percent of their decisions using these mental shortcuts or rules of thumb. They also emphasize the importance of framing and use of anecdotes to help people make decisions and filter events.

Behavioral economics, in contrast to traditional economics, has much to say about risk-taking.

In his 2016 book, *The Undoing Project: A Friendship That Changed Our Minds*, Michael Lewis describes the work done by the early behavioral economists Daniel Kahneman and Amos Tversky in the 1970s.[2] Their research uncovered a "Loss Aversion Bias," which essentially means people hate to lose. When facing a Moment of Truth, decision-makers often focus not on what they might win, but rather what they might lose. What we commonly think of as risk-averse people are focused on what they might lose if they take a particular risk, but successful risk-takers aren't just focused on potential gain from taking a risk, but *losses from avoiding risk*. Time and again we heard, "I didn't view my choice as that risky when I thought about what happened if I didn't take the risk."[3]

One of the risk-takers that we met, Fred Crosetto, moved to Taiwan after college simply because he read the book *Megatrends*, which predicted the economic growth of Asia. Fred created a successful safety glove business and now splits his time between Shanghai and Seattle. Fred's view of the cost of *not taking risks* has driven his decisions:

"If you're going to go out and swing the bat and you're going to strike out a little, do it when you're young," he says. "If you hit a home run, great. If you strike out, who cares? For a long time, the guy who hit the most home runs was Babe Ruth. He also struck out the most. Nobody sits around and talks about Babe Ruth striking out. I always looked at it more like if I *don't* do this, I'm going to be looking over my shoulder my entire life asking, 'What did I *not* do? I could have done that.'"

After Taiwan, Fred returned to Seattle and continued to build his safety glove business, renting a cheap office while going to law school. When he graduated, he decided to keep building the business rather than take a job with a fancy downtown law firm. As the business grew in Asia, he moved his whole family to Shanghai. Fred took risks at every turn, but the one thing he didn't risk was looking back at his life and regretting risks not taken.

Our research led us to this same universal truth about risk-taking, one that may seem self-contradictory at first glance. We found few people regret the risks they took that didn't work out, whether through clear failure or ambiguous results. Indeed, on many occasions, risk-takers told their stories of face-plants with relish and amusement. Especially as they age, interviewees regret much more the risky roads not taken, the times they played it safe (or thought they did), than their own flops and failures.

Repeatedly in our interviews, we noticed one particular perception. Even when taking extraordinary risks—spending money they didn't have, foregoing prestigious career options, leaving jobs that others would relish, asking significant others to understand the unthinkable—risk-takers focused on what they might lose by avoiding the risk, rather than the downsides of the actual risk. They thought more about, *What will I think at the end of my life if I never took this risk?* than they did about *What will happen to me if this risk doesn't work out?*

These choices about risk cannot be explained by conventional economic analyses. They are matters of both head and heart. While this shift in focus might seem subtle, it made a huge difference in the Moment of Truth decisions and the life trajectories of our risk-takers.

Livewith Three: Life *Is* Risk

We've all had times when we wanted to crawl under a rock or get a Starbucks and go back to bed. Unfortunately, even going back to bed can be risky when you consider muscular atrophy. It turns out there are no risk-free decisions in life. One of our interviewees escaped an abusive childhood in a West Virginia coal-mining town to eventually create a successful healthcare tech company, with his first stop at age fourteen being a Catholic seminary. He puts it this way: "Life is risk."

This realization has huge implications for how we think about risk. People encountering a risky situation often frame it as "Option A is changing and therefore taking a risk," and "Option B is not changing and therefore not taking a risk." However, nothing stays the same for long.

All of life is risky, but we don't always see it that way.

Livewith Four: Risk Never Fails to Teach

Even though risk-takers freely and openly acknowledge their mistakes and failures, they don't spend much time looking back—no matter their stage of life. We've all met people who wallow in regret and indulge in what-ifs, whose clock stops well before their life ends. Risk-takers are nothing like this. Instead, they are always looking for the next hill to climb, the next risk to take. Risk-takers learn from their experiences and move on.

Michael Frank, a neuroscientist at Brown University, studies how the brain responds to risky circumstances. He has concluded that "when you're in a situation with risk, the learning signals in your brain are stronger. The way in which people get better at things, at anything, is to take some risks and constantly change the level of expectation."[4]

Being in high-risk situations makes you more mentally alive, which is perhaps why those who have taken great risks reminisce fondly about such decisions. As Malcolm Gladwell described in his bestselling book, *The Tipping Point*, people get better at anything, including risk-taking, with deliberate practice.[5]

Whatever the outcome of a particular risk, the evidence is clear that conscious risk-taking yields learning and personal growth. Indeed, even when the risk doesn't work out, successful risk-takers have no regrets. They view their failures as essential to leading them to better decisions—and a better life.

Livewith Five: Risk Tastes Different with Age

Brain researchers have also substantiated what may be intuitive: how one views risk changes as you go through life.

Radboud University risk researcher Bernd Figner finds we take fewer risks as we get older. And the reasons, he argues, are twofold.

"There is a maturation of the prefrontal cortex that is happening well into young adulthood that enables us to be better at inhibiting our most influential responses—that is one important thing," he says. "But you also see these changes because you are more experienced. You now have these experiences, and you start to realize it's not always a good idea to take so many great risks. You understand the consequences better. You realize what's at stake."

A study that looked at risky behaviors in experienced rock climbers found that even experienced individuals tended to scale back on riskier climbs as they age.[6] This is supported by the work of Tversky and Kahneman; if people primarily think about "loss avoidance" when making Moment of Truth decisions, we have more to lose as we age. Many people view their twenties as a period of exploration; the same cannot be said of our forties and fifties, when life's demands have accumulated.

We believe, though, that something else is occurring. Daniel Kahneman, in his book, *Thinking, Fast and Slow*, identified two "systems of thinking." In System 1, we make "fast, intuitive, and emotional decisions," based on what we think of as "gut feel."

We observed many such System 1 decisions, significant ones, during our interviews. But they tended to happen earlier in interviewees' lives. You'll soon meet Andrew White, who, when he needed money to fund a business, put his house up for sale but forgot to tell his wife. This is a clear System 1 decision.

Kahneman describes another form of thinking, which he calls System 2, as "slower, more deliberative and logical." He argues that both forms of decision-making are necessary and important.

It seems that we don't lose the ability to make fast and intuitive decisions as we age. Instead, we balance that more often with slower and more logical decision-making, in part to avoid losing what we have—but also to make better decisions. Fred Crosetto put it this way: "You think about things more as you get older, as you get married, have kids, have more employees. Are you taking the same risks? The risks are always there, but you think differently."

Livewith Six: Mission Transforms Risk

You will soon meet Kirk Craig, who grew up in a wealthy environment. Kirk now lives in inner-city Houston with his wife and two children, where he created a faith-based nonprofit focused on vocational education and training for inner-city youth. Kirk acknowledges that he's chosen to locate his family in a neighborhood with a higher crime rate, but he takes precautions and has a bigger mission.

Time and again, we met individuals driven by a force beyond themselves.

We learned that a mission to contribute to something outside oneself can override other factors. What looks like a huge risk from the outside doesn't even feel like a risk to the person making the leap.

Having such a mission seemed to benefit the risk-taker, increasing the probability of success. People on missions tended to view obstacles as interesting rather than insurmountable.

As the Scottish athlete W. H. Murray said, "Whatever you can do, or dream you can, begin it. Boldness has genius, power, and magic in it."

CHAPTER THREE

The Risk-Takers

Like all of us, risk-takers are complicated. They frequently do not fully understand their motives, at least not in the risk-taking moment. Many times, they commented how valuable the interviews were to gain insights into their own past motives.

We came to understand the most distinctive and important part of the risk-taker story was not in the risk details or even the personalities and circumstances. The most critical part was the *why* of the risk-taker—their fundamental driver to take that first step into the unknown.

If someone understands *why* they are taking the risk, they can sustain nearly any of the *how* and *what to do next* challenges that inevitably arise. Motivation and purpose become the galvanizing force to get through the tough times. But if the risk-taker loses track of the *why* in the face of these obstacles, they are in trouble. Risk-taking does not reward hesitancy in the midst of the challenge.

From our research, we observed six primary categories of risk-takers:

Idealists

Idealists are driven to make a "dent in the universe," as Steve Jobs famously said. They have a vision of how the world should be, they understand the world is not as it should be, and they believe they can close that gap. Their risk is in making that vision happen. Often, they start by trying to change the world from inside an organization, but they become frustrated by the challenges. Their intense desire to make the world better motivates them to make the leap.

Adventurers

Several risk-takers were primarily driven by adventure, almost like risk-junkies. These Adventurers take on multiple risks over a lifetime and move quickly from one situation to the next. Their purpose seems to be the adventure itself, and they tend not to be introspective. They are too busy seeking out adventure to spend much time looking back or inward. They typically respond to failure, even catastrophic ones, simply by seeking the next adventure.

Liberators

Some risk-takers take big risks to escape the day-to-day grind of corporate life, to be their own boss, for the chance to live their own dream. These folks are motivated by avoiding the bureaucracy and depersonalization of corporate life. They have an overwhelming desire for independence. They frequently discover other motivations once they leap into their own venture. They are essentially solo practitioners.

Survivors

Several risk-takers experienced an incredibly challenging life event. Often, an event that would crush someone else or at least cause them to seek safe harbor. Instead, these individuals made a huge leap designed to improve their lives and the world in the process.

Seekers

We encountered those who accomplished significant financial success, only to discover that—money aside—they were no more fulfilled. This led to deeper searches for meaningful engagement in the world. They took significant risks in their search for meaning, including letting go of established reputations and valued relationships that became obstacles to their search.

Givers

Serving others can be a powerful motivator. Sometimes profound experiences in early life, even tragedies, shaped the life mission of risk-takers to serve others. Many risk-takers find that after material needs are met, their meaning manifests as a Giver.

These six categories of risk-takers demonstrate the Livewiths in their decision-making, although some categories manifest a particular Livewith more vividly. We will cover these dynamics as you meet them.

The stories that follow illustrate the power of these motivations, as well as the fascinating lives of people who take risks conventionally viewed as inadvisable.

CHAPTER FOUR

Idealists

Some risk-takers are driven by a vision of a better world. Yes, they want adventure and independence, but most essentially, they want to realize an ideal that makes a difference.

One phrase we heard repeatedly from such risk-takers was, "I can't *not* do it." Once they had their vision of how to change the world, they were compelled to pursue it, no matter the sacrifices.

Meriwether Lewis was an Idealist driven by a mission, one handed to him by Thomas Jefferson. In 1803, Jefferson announced the completion of the Louisiana Purchase, 825,000 square miles bought from Napoleon's France for $15 million.

Jefferson was convinced he struck a great deal to double the size of the country but was unsure of what he bought. He tapped thirty-three-year-old Lewis, his private secretary in the White House, to lead an exploration of the territory. Congress approved $2,500 for Lewis's supplies, and Jefferson handed Lewis an unlimited letter of credit, pledging the government to repay "citizens of any nation to furnish you with those supplies which your necessities may call for."

Lewis recruited his ex-military boss William Clark to join him to form the Lewis and Clark expedition. The mission was to reach the "western ocean" (the Pacific) via the Northwest Passage—a hypothetical, continuous waterway across the continent—and report back to Jefferson on the animal, vegetation, and geographic conditions along the route.

In the true spirit of an Idealist, Lewis decided to either "succeed or perish," but never turn around until his team reached the western ocean. Months passed with no communication from Lewis to Jefferson, amid rumors the entire expedition had been killed by "Indians."

In fact, Lewis and Clark were greatly aided by Native Americans. Where they expected the Northwest Passage waterway, they found the Rocky Mountains. Luckily, a sixteen-year-old girl from the Shoshone tribe, Sacagawea, had joined their journey and helped trade for the horses needed to scale the mountains.

On the other side of the mountains, Lewis and Clark faced a life-threatening choice on where to spend the winter. "They could remain on the north side of Columbia's mouth, though the Chinook Indians charged what Clark considered extravagant prices for everything." They could move to the south side (in what is now Oregon, which promised "plenty of elk for food and clothing. Or they could head back upriver . . . where they could count on drier weather."[7]

As former military commanders, Lewis and Clark made an unconventional decision: they put the decision to a vote. Clark's slave, York, was allowed to vote—nearly sixty years before slaves in America were emancipated. Sacagawea voted too—more than a century before either women or Indians were granted voting rights. The team decided to spend the winter on the south side of the Columbia River, and they all survived.

In late November 1805, more than two years after they began their mission, Lewis and Clark reached the Pacific Ocean, and Lewis reported back to Jefferson on his mission's survival and success:

"In obedience to your orders we have penetrated the Continent of North America to the Pacific Ocean and sufficiently explored the interior of the country to affirm with confidence that we have discovered the most practicable route which does exist . . ."[8]

Meriwether Lewis was an archetypal Idealist. More than others, Idealists are driven by Livewith Six: Mission Transforms Risk. They not only believe in their mission—they feel it in their bones.

Zoe Littlepage

"If we won the case, the firm would survive. If we lost, I would have to declare bankruptcy."

Zoe Littlepage was born in Trinidad. Her father, a Trinidadian, was an airline pilot for Pan American Airlines. Her mother, who was from Barbados, felt she was not appropriately challenged in school in the Caribbean, so when Zoe was twelve, she went to boarding school in England.

Zoe always knew she wanted to be a lawyer for a very simple reason. She says, "I really liked to talk. I had been on the debate team. I had been on the speech team. I was very comfortable on my feet. I couldn't think of a career where people would see you to talk other than politician and lawyer, and I didn't want to be a politician. It seemed like a great opportunity to go to law school and litigate and be in a courtroom."

Zoe went to law school at the University of Houston, then she took a job for one of the big, fancy defense firms in Houston. She hated it. She was working for insurance companies that would look for reasons not to pay when someone's house burned down, even though the homeowners had been paying their premiums for years. She didn't believe in what she was doing, which was always very important to her. Nevertheless, she stayed for a year, because otherwise she would have had to pay back her signing bonus.

Next, Zoe went to work for a small firm of plaintiff's attorneys in Houston. The firm was conservative and hardly believed in business cards, let alone advertising. They thought that all lawyers who advertised were scummy.

Zoe thought that silicone breast implants, popular at the time, were a very bad idea. She wanted to run a TV ad to find women in Houston who had been harmed by them. When she asked to run an ad in Houston, her firm said, "No way." But they let her run one in Dallas . . . with a very modest budget.

The budget was so tiny that Zoe could only hire one model who sat in front of a blank screen and said the following words: "I had silicone breast implants. I'm having these health problems. If you are having the same problems, call this 800 number." They ran the ad ten times in Dallas and got a huge response. Within four months, Zoe had two hundred clients, which was double the client count of the rest of the firm.

Zoe's success caused jealousy and resentment, and it didn't help that she was the only woman. After two years, the firm made her a partner, a promotion that normally takes eight to ten years for a young lawyer. But six months later, at her first partnership meeting, they reneged on the financial terms of her partnership agreement. They said to Zoe, "You know that partnership agreement you signed six months ago that gave you a certain percentage in your cases? We did the math and you have more cases than anybody else. If that partnership agreement stands, you would make a huge amount of money. So, we are going to keep the same partnership deal for all the rest of us, but we're going to cut yours."

Many young lawyers, male or female, would have simply gone home and cried that night. Instead, Zoe went to dinner with the oldest attorney at the firm, Sid, who was about ready to retire. They talked about how unfair the firm had been to her. Zoe told Sid that she didn't think she could stay and work for these people, that she couldn't live with it. Sid said, "Well, if you leave, I will leave with you."

Zoe went home that night and called a friend who said she could set up an office in their conference room. The conference room was actually more like a closet, within the friend's office. At 11:00 p.m. that night, she went into the law firm's office and took all of her files. She called Sid at 1:00 a.m. and told him where their new "office" was. Sid and Zoe worked together for the next couple of years, through the conclusion of the breast implant cases, and then Zoe took over the firm on her own.

> **LESSON LEARNED:** Risk-takers use
> personal disasters as opportunities.

Right after Zoe started her own firm, Alan met her in Houston. In fact, Zoe was Alan's first professional employer. Here's how Alan remembers it:

"I graduated from Rice University and was staying in Houston for the summer before I started med school in Columbus, Ohio.

I was living with friends, and I needed to support myself. This was 1994, so there were still bulletin boards. I saw a five-by-seven card with handwriting on it seeking legal assistance for a medical litigation firm. I called them up and interviewed.

"There were only two people at the interview. A young paralegal and Zoe, a sprightly blonde woman with huge blue eyes and a permanent smile who looked barely older than me. I was hired on the spot. I asked them, 'Okay, what am I going to do?' They said, 'You're going to be our medical liaison.'

"I show up to work, and it was clear that we were using someone else's office. I worked in a room that was maybe 200 square feet, and there were four people in that room. I don't even think all those other people worked for Zoe.

"Zoe was all energy and so helpful and so smart, and she just threw me into stuff. There would be meetings with thousands of women who were her clients for breast implant litigation. I didn't have a tie. I had to borrow a tie. I had to review documents for medical terminology. I knew nothing. I was a philosophy major and undergrad who happened to be going to med school. This is all just in three months of work."

Zoe found her calling as a plaintiff's lawyer, going up against some of the biggest and wealthiest corporations in America. She felt her client's pain and anguish, which made her an extremely effective advocate for them. But the work of a plaintiff attorney was not easy. You only make money on contingency, and you don't get your cash until your clients have theirs. Generally speaking, even when you are successful, you won't settle your client's cases until years after you start working the case.

Zoe borrowed $50,000 from her parents to get the firm off the ground. She paid herself and Sid very little. Then she got to work.

"I don't think I ever really thought I was going to walk out three years after law school with nothing and start my own firm. I guess I thought I would work for a plaintiffs' firm. How plaintiffs' firms work is that everybody gets big bonuses, so you see a lot of young lawyers leave after the end of the first litigation when they get a $50,000 bonus or a $25,000 bonus or a $75,000 bonus. And they take that bonus to start their own firm. It didn't work out for me because I didn't anticipate that they would try and screw me on the partnership, and I would have to leave in the middle of the night and start the firm with nothing. But I did and thank God my parents were there."

Zoe and Sid started winning some of the silicone breast implant cases. Soon after those cases began to settle, Zoe started working on fen-phen litigation. Fenfluramine/phentermine, aka fen-phen, was an anti-obesity treatment proven to cause potentially fatal pulmonary hypertension and heart valve issues.

The fen-phen cases were progressing well when Zoe ran into a big problem. One of the major manufacturers of fen-phen, Dow Corning, went into bankruptcy, which protected them from paying out litigation. That was a huge hit for Zoe and her firm, because they had numerous Dow Corning cases and were counting on settlements from fen-phen. That's when Sid decided that he needed to leave the partnership, due to the financial risks. Now, Zoe was on her own and the survival of the firm was at stake.

As if that stress wasn't enough, she also just had her first child. She remembers, "I was bringing him to work and putting him in a box under my desk so that he didn't have the fluorescent lights in his eyes, while I prepared for the trial (with Wyeth, one of the key manufacturers of fen-phen). The day I left for trial, my dad came and picked up my six-week-old son and flew him home to be with him and my mom while I went to court.

"I was carrying all these fen-phen cases, which had a lot of costs, a lot of expense. It was make-or-break. If we won the case, the firm would survive. If we lost, all the money I had to borrow to invest in it would be gone, and I would have to declare bankruptcy.

"We loaded up my car; strapped boxes to the roof; and me, two young lawyers, and two young legal assistants stuffed ourselves into it. We drove all the way from Houston to small-town Council Bluffs, Iowa, to take on Wyeth in a courtroom.

"We arrive there, and we've rented a one-bedroom unfurnished apartment. We have blow-up beds and folding tables and chairs. We set up our stuff and go to our first meeting with Wyeth. They have rented the entire four-story Carnegie Library downtown and moved in their legal team. I'm our only lawyer. I show up to the meeting alone straight from a one-bedroom apartment with a blow-up bed and folding table and chairs.

"We picked the jury and that went well. I was there by myself at counsel table. It was good optics. Here's a young female lawyer against nine of Wyeth's lawyers. We had a good judge. We've got a good jury. My client was really good. I put the first witness on and then it came to the weekend. Saturday morning, Wyeth called and said, 'We have flown in settlement counsel. We'd like to meet with you.' I met with settlement counsel that afternoon. And on Sunday morning, they settled half of my fen-phen cases and made me a multimillionaire."

Zoe had her first pot of money that she could use to build the firm. She had just turned thirty years old.

Zoe was having a blast, but she was also terrified. She was living on the edge of fear and exhilaration. She was totally committed to her clients. In several of her cases, she refused settlements that would have dug her out of huge financial holes because she didn't believe the settlement was enough for her clients. She loved going up against the many, gray-suited defense lawyers on the other side of the courtroom. She genuinely believed she was up against evil companies that needed to be punished. She also possessed a deep-seated belief that she was going to win, she was going to find a way through.

It's what Zoe did next that is truly amazing.

Many people would have taken their money, millions of dollars at thirty years old, and gone home. Zoe isn't one of those people. She next plunged into hormone replacement therapy cases, which dragged on for more than twelve years. The drug companies were experts at bleeding litigation attorneys to death. At one point, she was $7 million in debt on the new litigation.

> **LESSON LEARNED:** For risk-takers, adversity
> does not build character, it reveals character.

"By the end of the hormone therapy cases, I was under real stress," Zoe recalls. "My hair was falling out. I was thinking about how crazy it was to do this. But on the other side, we were doing great work. Some of the best legal work I have ever done, some of the finest trials, some of the worthiest plaintiffs. I loved my clients.

"I really knew the company we were up against was bad, bad, bad. What they had done was just outrageous. We were going up against the best lawyers in the country, really complicated, complex legal issues, medical issues. We were kicking their ass. It was exhilarating, but the stress was tough. By then I'm thinking, *Am I going to have to go into my kids' college funds? Am I going to have to start over again in my forties and go back to work for someone else?*

"The last couple of years of the hormone therapy case, we were on a shoestring budget. I had to fire everybody, shut down the office, and move everything into my house. I sold my dining room table and chairs, and I put a couple of desks in my kitchen and living room. I had a couple of part-timers so I didn't have to pay benefits. It was very stressful, but also very enjoyable. We were doing great, amazing, legal work."

Zoe just kept fighting for her clients no matter the pressure involved. She risked her entire livelihood and the financial security of her family for her ideals, her purpose. Finally, after twelve years—4,380 days—the case broke her way.

"I'm working all the time, seven days a week, twenty hours a day. I'm putting everything into it. We're going to mediators and they're offering money. Good money, but not enough for my clients. Every time I go to mediation, I think, *Okay, this is it. This is the time.* And they just wouldn't offer enough money for my clients, and we'd have to walk away. It was more than enough money to save the firm, but that's not what mattered. What mattered is what all the clients are getting paid fairly.

"I'd go to mediation with all these hopes and then they would be dashed. Then I'd go to mediation again, four, six months later. They'd offer a little bit more. Still not enough. I'd go back to trial, back-to-back trials. I'm dead tired, working for weeks around the clock. I'd go back to mediation. They move a little, but not a lot.

"And then finally, October of 2012, we went to mediation where they finally offered enough money that we could take it. We got more money for our clients than any other law firm in the country, and it was the fair amount of money. I just held out until they paid my clients what I thought they deserved."

Zoe's firm settled almost a thousand cases in one afternoon—the money was the largest settlement of a medical malpractice suit in history. Suddenly, the work and the stress disappeared, and she got a huge pot of money after the clients received their settlements.

Zoe now had enough money that, for the first time in her life, she could take time off. She worked "very part time" for the next four years. She taught at a law school, consulted on other cases, and traveled. After her son graduated from college, she realized she missed the excitement and energy of practicing her work full time. Recently, in her early fifties, she re-opened her law firm—and she was soon overwhelmed with clients.

We asked Zoe, looking back, how she viewed her original career risks: "I thought I was going to win. I thought I was going to win big. And then I could borrow against the verdict and keep the firm going long enough to take the case on appeal. I recognized if we lost, I was done, but I liked my case. I liked my clients. I thought the companies we were up against were terrible and deserved to be punished. I thought I was going to win, and I was having fun. I mean, it's kind of fun to show up in Iowa and be the one person against the army of gray-suited lawyers in the courtroom. Yes, I did realize it was a tremendous gamble."

Yet Zoe also has a fascinating personal dimension in how she views risk, which at first blush appears to be a contradiction. While she has clearly taken enormous risks in her legal practice, she is conservative when it comes to managing her own personal money. She's bought a lot of real estate, and she always pays cash. She has never taken on credit card debt. It's as if she can only deal with so much risk, so she limits her risk-taking to her legal practice. We found this same pattern with several risk-takers that we interviewed.

Peter Kash

"Knowing your weaknesses, and not being ashamed of them, is actually a strength."

Peter Kash grew up in Brooklyn. His parents were first-generation immigrants from Poland and Russia. They had come from poor families. During childhood, he slept in the kitchen, while his three sisters slept in one bed and his parents in another.

Peter started working when he was ten, buying vegetable seeds at a local landscaping place and selling them to the neighbors. Eventually he moved onto a newspaper route. When he was sixteen, Peter started selling bumper stickers at concerts and making $1,000 a night. He never actually went to any of the concerts, he just got a peddler's license and sold stickers in the parking lot.

Peter was a long-distance runner, and when he was seventeen he developed a knee problem. He invented a knee brace using Velcro, and he even got venture capital invested in the product. He tried to sell the product through the largest knee brace manufacturer in North America, but negotiations didn't progress. Six months later, the manufacturer released a similar product, and he realized they had stolen his idea. Peter says with zero bitterness, "I learned that business is not always nice. It was a great lesson. It was my entrée into understanding about business dealings with other people."

In college, Peter sold perfume on consignment from someone who would get damaged packages from Bloomingdales and Macy's. He did well enough around Christmas and Valentine's Day to fund ski trips for two years. Peter worked all these jobs because he understood that asking his parents for five or ten dollars was out of the question; they simply didn't have it.

After college, Peter got a summer internship with the brokerage firm EF Hutton, but after graduation he decided instead to live on a kibbutz in Israel for eighteen months. He loved his work on the kibbutz and even served in the Israeli military for eighteen months after that. His mom wasn't happy because she felt he wasn't using his college degree, but Peter loved being in Israel. And he wanted to see more of the world.

When he returned to the United States, he earned an MBA, funded by EF Hutton, and then took a job in healthcare venture capital. "That's exactly what I wanted to do," he says. "Something in healthcare and science, playing a supporting role to doctors and scientists. That's what I've been doing ever since."

Peter didn't make a salary in his first venture capital job; he was paid only in equity. By then he was married, but his wife advised him to take the job because of the upside opportunity, plus she was making good money at the time.

Peter was successful in the early stages of his healthcare tech investing career, if it's possible to say that someone is successful without making much money for himself. He drove early-stage investments in three biotech companies that went public and achieved market valuations of over $1 billion, but all three of them crashed due to a combination of regulatory and management problems before he could cash out his stock position. He couldn't sell his stock position soon enough because his employer would not let him, and he wasn't on the board of any of the three companies.

In 2004, Peter went off on his own with two partners to create a small healthcare investment bank. He says it wasn't as big a deal to start out on his own as it would be for most people. "When you start with nothing, you can't go too far down. That's the beauty of not growing up with a silver spoon: you don't fear failure. I know what it's like living with very little. To me, the concept of fear and risk never entered the picture."

> **LESSON LEARNED:** Those who start with nothing often feel they have nothing to lose.

The origins of the next phase of Peter's career go back to very early in his life.

"I can tell you exactly when my purpose was born. It was June 1968, and I was seven years old. We were playing hide-and-seek in Long Island at about five o'clock at night.

"There was a young girl named Mary Ellen O'Bryan who lived up the street. She was six years old. She was running, and then suddenly, her wig fell off, leaving her totally bald. At that age, you never saw a boy who was bald, let alone a girl who was bald. Unfortunately, we started to laugh because we were children, and we didn't know how to react. She ran inside. It was explained to us that she had something called cancer. Pediatric leukemia. She passed several months later."

This experience gave purpose to Peter's entire life and career. Initially, he wanted to be a doctor, but he decided in school that he just didn't have the aptitude for medicine. Nor was he a scientist. Could it be possible to pursue his passion for science in a different way?

"I loved science . . . but I realized I did not have those skill sets, which was a great thing. Knowing my weaknesses at a young age allowed me to amplify my strengths, where most people don't learn that until later in life. Knowing your weaknesses, and not being ashamed of them, is actually a strength."

Peter's healthcare investment bank was successful. Successful enough that seven years later, in 2011, he decided to leave and become completely independent. He is now a founding board member of a targeted immunotherapy company based in Switzerland, with much of their core research being done in Israel. He's been working for the last thirty years with small biotech companies that develop unique therapeutic compounds to treat and cure diseases, mainly in oncology. In other words, he's trying to cure cancer. Specifically, solid tumor cancers (such as colon cancer) rather than blood cancers.

"The first drug I got approved by the FDA when I was a co-founder of a biotech firm was arsenic trioxide. It was the first drug ever approved from China by the US FDA. To me, that was the biggest highlight of my life. I was not the scientist, but I was a co-founder of this company that produced arsenic trioxide from China. The specific lead indication (use of the drug) was pediatric leukemia. I can't explain to you that high, from 1968 to thirty-five years later, that I got from having a drug approved specifically for pediatric cancer. I can't explain it. That is when I realized my purpose."

In creating the targeted immunotherapy company, Peter applied two of the key lessons he's learned in business. One is that less is more. "I gave up a lot of equity ownership in order to recruit the team," he says. "Nothing has to be equal, but everything has to be equitable, which is my favorite line." Secondly, he is a strong believer in bringing people smarter than yourself onto the team, and not having an ego about it. He was the CEO when he started the company but stepped down from that role when he found the right person to run it. Then he was the board chairman, but again stepped down when he found someone else better suited to the role. So now, he is vice chairman, while being active in the company on a day-to-day basis.

As Peter reflects on his success, he emphasizes the importance of purpose. "The single most important thing I've learned in my life is to have a purpose. My purpose is nailing cancer. That is my main purpose in life. You don't have to win the Oscars. You can get a supporting Oscar role by being a groupie, like people are groupies to rock stars. Well, I'm a groupie to scientists. I get to hang out with some of the brightest minds in the world. For me, it's the greatest high in the world. It's a purpose."

With great emotion, Peter makes it clear how important his own family has been in his journey. "To be honest with you, it's my wife and my children that gave me the strength. They were so supportive. They sacrificed so many weekends with me not being there. It was really my family that gave me the support and the confidence, especially my children. They realized that it was not just a business I was doing. It was a purpose."

Peter was picking up all of his children for a weekend trip when he was interviewed for this book. We noticed that he took the time to introduce each of them and explain what they were currently doing in life. As he did this, it was entirely clear how much Peter supported his children, just as they have supported him.

Evan Marwell

"As my wife says, I'm the great actualizer. I like having an idea and I actually do it, whereas most people have ideas that they don't do anything about."

Evan Marwell grew up in Madison, Wisconsin. His father was a professor of sociology, and his mother was a school psychologist in Madison Public Schools.

Evan's mom always said that nothing ever really phases him. He is an optimist by nature. When he was thirteen, his father went on sabbatical for a year to a small English town called Colchester, taking the family with him. It was Evan's first risk-taking experience. "I was probably the first American that had ever shown up in the lives of my English peers," he recalls. "It was an extraordinary growth experience for me: learning how to adapt, how to integrate, how to deal with the challenges of being the new person in an uncomfortable situation." The good news was that the English girls loved his American accent, and he says this was the peak of his lifelong dating experience, at age thirteen.

In the summer after his sophomore year of high school, Evan went to Penn State to participate in a National Science Foundation Summer Research Program. He was fascinated by how science and technology could potentially change the world—an interest that has stuck with him throughout his life.

Evan went to Harvard thinking he would major in molecular biology, but then he realized he was going to be asked to spend his whole college career memorizing stuff. That didn't interest him. Instead, he became an economics major, and he stayed interested in technology.

Evan has always been comfortable with making unconventional career choices. He focuses on learning and growth much more than personal brand-building. When he left Harvard, he decided to work in management consulting. But he turned down offers from the big brand-name management consulting firms.

"The first risk I took in my life was when I came out of college, and I went into management consulting. I had offers from McKinsey and BCG and Bain and all the big guys, but I went to this little firm called Corporate Decisions, which had started two years earlier by four guys who had just made partner at Bain and then decided to spin out their own company. I chose that over going to McKinsey. People were like, "Are you nuts?" But I didn't feel like I needed the McKinsey brand, and I was going to get more responsibility here. So, no I didn't think this was a risk. I didn't think it would be a failure."

LESSON LEARNED: Idealists seek learning first.

Evan doesn't think of himself as a born entrepreneur—he is driven neither by adventure nor the need for independence. Instead, he is very open to opportunity and not afraid to pursue compelling opportunities when they arise.

After three years in management consulting, Evan went to Harvard Business School. Upon graduation, he had all the career possibilities that MBA students from the top schools get—management consulting, investment banking, consumer marketing.

He turned them all down. He was one of the three members of his graduating class who started a business right after graduation.

That business idea came to Evan after an excessively high phone bill. "During my second year in business school, I was living with four guys all doing job searches, and 411 was free in Boston. We were using 411 like it was going out of style. One day, they started charging, but nobody knew. Our phone bill came in that month, and it had gone from $30 to $130. I was like, 'What the heck is going on here?' We had a roommate from England, so I figured he must've made some long calls to England. And then I saw that we had a $100 bill for 411."

The phone companies were charging for 411 directory assistance but Evan knew all the phone directories were publicly available on CD-ROM. He realized that there were no barriers to starting a business, opening a call center, and competing with the phone companies. He and a friend from Harvard sized up the market potential for 411 services at around $3 billion per year.

Evan and his friend researched what it would take to get the call center off the ground, and how to secure the phone directories to support the 411 service. Being in New York City, they started targeting the financial services industry as customers for their new service.

Then came their first big break. "We found this guy at Merrill Lynch who was pissed off at the phone company. He didn't care about saving money on 411, but he cared about shoving it to the phone company, and this was a good way he could do that. He said, 'If you build this thing, I will be your first customer.' With that commitment, we were able to close a million-dollar investment round, and get the product built. Then, we were able to go serve him. That was the beginning of it all."

The financial services business was a great early adopter market for Evan's company. "If someone at Merrill Lynch picked up the phone and called 411, they'd ask for, generally speaking, a restaurant or a strip club. It was like that. Those are probably the two biggest calls that we got.

"So, we went out, opened a call center. We were living in New York City, but we opened the call center in Easton, Pennsylvania, because you can't run a call center in New York City. We would drive every day seventy-eight miles across the state of New Jersey from New York City to Easton, Pennsylvania. We had three call center operators to begin with, and my partner and I were numbers four and five when it got busy.

"If someone dialed 411, the phone system at Merrill Lynch would reprogram it and send it to our number. We would answer the call, use our software to find them the number, then that was that."

Their second big break came from a new market opportunity, without which Evan says they would not have been nearly as successful: the cell phone companies and public adoption of mobile phones during the 1990s.

The cell phone companies became huge customers. There were massive challenges getting the technology to support automated 411 assistance, which gave the consumer the option to ring through to the targeted number, but Evan and his partner persevered.

By 1998 Evan had grown bored with the operationally intensive business. He is a builder, but not the kind of person to optimize an existing operation. With the business at over $100 million in revenue, Evan was able to extract some life-changing money, north of $5 million, and still keep some equity in the business, which he has retained to this day.

Evan and his partner had another idea for a customer relationship management (CRM) software company. He raised over $30 million in venture capital funding for the start-up, and there was another round of funding sitting on his desk to sign off on September 11, 2001. After the tragedy that morning was Evan's Moment of Truth. He decided to turn down the money because he no longer believed they could make the business work in the post-9/11 world.

"I've got my series B financing sitting on my desk. I go to my board, which was largely who put up the series B financing. I say, 'You shouldn't give me this money. I think it's going to be nuclear winter for small software companies. I think this money will last us for two years, and we'll make progress, but we're not going to make enough progress, and you're going to have to write another check. As the founder, part of my job is to be the steward of your capital, and I think this is a bad use of your capital, so you shouldn't give it to me.' They just looked at me, stunned, and said, 'Nobody's ever said that to us. So, okay. If that's what you think the right answer is.'"

Evan says admitting that failure was the hardest thing he's ever done. The venture capital guys were shocked that he didn't take the money.

LESSON LEARNED: Idealists do the right thing, even when it's not personally beneficial.

On the heels of this failure, a friend of Evan's who lived in San Francisco called and asked if he wanted to start a hedge fund. The friend was already in the hedge fund business, and he thought Evan would be a good hedge fund manager even though he didn't have experience in the industry. Evan presented his wife with two options: travel around the world for a year with their three children or go to San Francisco to start a hedge fund. Evan's wife is not a financial risk-taker. They moved to San Francisco in early 2003.

Evan and his partner each put $2 million into the hedge fund. Seven years later, in 2010, the hedge fund was up to $1.4 billion in assets, and everyone had made a ton of money. This took Evan back to the issue that he doesn't like to run an existing operation. He was bored again.

For the first time in his life, Evan took time to dig deep and explore what he wanted to do next. He started writing a blog but discovered he didn't like that. He looked at a few new business ideas but realized he didn't want to start another business—at least not then.

Evan went to some seminars and got some coaching on his life purpose. He realized his purpose was to be a change-maker—in other words, to work on changing the world. He began to fully understand his skill at getting things off the ground, at actualizing ideas. And, as he puts it, "If your purpose is to be a change-maker, risk is part of the game."

Evan was clear on what he was willing to risk. He decided he was willing to risk his time to work on implementing big ideas that might not work—as long as they were worthwhile. And he was willing to risk his reputation, since he'd already experienced failure and realized that it was survivable. But he wasn't willing to risk his family's financial security.

Evan started looking around for big ideas to actualize.

"I read a book called *Bold Endeavors* by Felix G. Rohatyn. He was the Chairman of Lazard and was the guy who saved New York City from bankruptcy back in the seventies. He wrote this book making the argument that we need an infrastructure bank to get us out of the Great Recession. The book was basically ten vignettes of similar infrastructure projects. I think Erie Canal, Transcontinental Railroad, Rural Electrification were in there—changes that altered the face of America. His point was only the government is big enough to do these things.

"When I read the book, the other thing I took away was that behind every one of those projects was a guy who had some crazy vision and kept at it and kept at it and kept at it until the government showed up with the money. I'd done a lot of self-reflection about what I loved to do. I knew I loved being an entrepreneur coming up with ideas. I'm very good strategically. I love being an evangelist. As my wife says, I'm the great actualizer. I like having an idea and then actually doing it, whereas most people have ideas that they don't do anything about."

> **LESSON LEARNED:** Great risk-takers understand what they are great at.

Evan was on the board of his daughter's charter school in San Francisco. He had solved a tech problem for the teachers when he realized their internet access was through an obsolete modem. He got the school to upgrade to a Wi-Fi network, and suddenly the teachers were happy.

"Then I get invited to the White House in January 2012 to meet with fifteen CEOs and entrepreneurs from Silicon Valley and talk about how to make America better with technology. I'm like, 'What the hell am I going to talk about?' Then I thought, *If my daughter's private school in the heart of Silicon Valley has lousy internet, I wonder what it's like in public schools across the country?* I looked and looked, and I couldn't really find any data, but then I found this survey by the Federal Communications Commission. It said 80 percent of schools had lousy broadband. I thought, *Perfect. This is what I'm going to talk about at the White House.*

"At the White House we're sitting in this conference room when this guy, Aneesh Chopra, who was the Chief Technology Officer of the United States at the time, comes in. He gives a little speech and starts going around the table. He says, 'Okay, what should we do?' He gets to me and I said, 'Oh, we should fix the school broadband problem.' He looks at me and he says, 'What school broadband problem? All our schools have broadband. We have this program called E-Rate. We spend $2.4 billion a year to fund it.'

"He finishes going around the table and then President Obama arrives. Aneesh sits down next to me. The President starts giving his speech and then he starts going around the table. Aneesh leans over to me and says, 'Hey, you should go fix that.' I said, 'Fix what?' He said, 'That school broadband problem.' I said, 'I thought we're here to tell you what to fix!'

"Aneesh says, 'Let me tell you a secret. With the government, we don't fix anything. We have no capacity to fix anything. We have a bully pulpit, we can make policy, we have funding, but we can't actually go do anything. So, you should go fix it.'"

The book *Bold Endeavors,* the trip to the White House, and Evan's own self-reflection on his life purpose as a change-maker was enough inspiration. In January 2012, Evan started a nonprofit called Education Superhighway, with the focused and explicit goal to get fast broadband access in all schools.

The results have been amazing. Through a connection from his mom back in Wisconsin, Evan realized that each state's Department of Education was the critical force in widespread adoption of broadband. He persuaded President Obama to announce a national broadband initiative.

"Essentially, our work has gone in three phases. Phase one was raise awareness. That's what we did with this National School Speed Test. Phase two was to fix the policy and get the resources. We then spent two years working with the FCC to change this E-Rate program that provides the money. We ended up phasing out that billion dollars a year being spent on phone service, shifting it to broadband, and then they added another billion and a half dollars. We went from $1.4 billion to $3.9 billion a year of funding for broadband in schools, plus we changed a bunch of other things in the program, giving schools more options on how to buy, which was important for competition. Critically, we convinced them to make all the data about who is buying what, and from whom, public.

"Phase three was actually working with the schools to get upgrades, which started in 2015. And then we realized we needed a distribution channel and that the State Department of Education had been our distribution channel for speed tests, but we had to go higher up in the organization if we wanted to get the upgrades done. So, we went after governors and said, 'Hey, we're going to do this report on the national state of broadband in every public school in America. To win you need good data on who has broadband in your state. By the way, none of you have good data, so you should commit to fixing this problem publicly.' We got thirty-four governors to commit to upgrading the broadband in their public schools in that first year. That set us on our way.

"In 2013, when we had our first data, 4 million out of the 47 million kids in public schools actually had decent broadband in their classrooms. As of the start of this past school year, we were up to 45 million out of the 47 million. We will be at 99 percent of these kids by the start of the next school year. And then we will shut down."

In the space of seven years, Evan has taken an important national education problem, solved it, and now he is close to working his way out of a job.

And he is unworried about finding his next mission for changing the world.

> **LESSON LEARNED:** Ambitious missions can drive risk-takers to almost disregard risk.

Judi Sheppard Missett

"Don't think about the negative stuff. Think about what could happen. Listen to what that voice inside tells you."

Judi Sheppard Missett was born in San Diego, but she moved to Red Oak, Iowa, when she was three. A doctor told her mom that Judi was pigeon-toed, and it would probably help if she went to dance class to correct that defect.

"Mom sought out dance teachers and found a class in Shenandoah. From the minute I walked through that door, dance was my love. I knew it was the most important thing I could do with my life. I never had a question about what I was going to do. It was always going to involve dancing in one way or another.

"My mom was very supportive, got me to classes, practiced with me, made costumes for me for recitals. When my dance teacher decided to go back to Council Bluffs where she had a larger studio, my mom recruited dance teachers to come to our small town. She found some good instructors who were young and wanted to develop a business of their own. She would help them find facilities, set up their business, be their studio manager, and help produce the recitals. Basically, she was an integral part in what they were doing for no other reason than to facilitate me having good instruction—and other kids too, because there were a lot of kids interested in dance."

By time Judi was thirteen, her parents had turned their basement into a dance studio, and Judi was teaching classes for a hundred other kids at two dollars per child per class. Judi's mom was still driving her to Omaha, two hours round trip, for her own dance lessons.

Judi decided to major in theater at college. As she was trying to decide between Stanford and Northwestern, a famous jazz dance teacher, Gus Giordano, visited Omaha to teach some classes. When Gus saw how talented Judi was, he convinced her to come to Northwestern.

LESSON LEARNED: Many risk-takers have influential mentors in their lives.

Gus had a studio in Evanston, Illinois, near Northwestern's campus. When Judi started college, she took as many classes as she could from Gus. He helped her get an agent and secure roles in theater shows, which helped her fund college since Northwestern was expensive.

After graduating, Judi stayed in Evanston. She met her husband-to-be on a blind date, and was teaching jazz dance classes at Gus's studio, mostly to housewives. Judi loved teaching the classes, but for some reason the housewives weren't sticking with the class. Judi wondered why.

"I thought, *Well, I'm just going to ask them. I'll do a little interview.* I called some of them up and I said, 'I noticed that you haven't been in class. I'm wondering if there's anything that I was doing that offended you?' Every single one of them said, 'No. The class was great. You're a great teacher, but it's too hard. It's too disciplined. You're teaching it like we're going to go on to Broadway. We don't want to be a professional dancer. We just want to look like one. We want to have the body and the endurance and the physical appearance of one.' I thought, *Wow, I never even thought about that.* They continued, 'We want to look like you.' I thought, *Okay, well, I can do that.*

"So, I asked Gus if I could have an empty studio. He said that I could. He was a risk-taker all his life too. I said, 'I have this idea for a class that would be different than a strict jazz dance class. I just want to try it for these people. I'll get in touch with them, let them know what I'm doing, and let's just see what happens.'"

Judi realized her students wanted a healthy, fun, nonthreatening place to move their bodies. She turned the mirrors so that the women couldn't see themselves and chose music that was on the radio and easy to follow. She put small flyers in stores around town where women would shop.

Judi held her classes on Thursday night at seven. She had fifteen people in her first class. Then she had thirty the next week and sixty the week after that.

It was the late 1960s in Chicago, and Judi's husband was a news reporter for CBS television. The political environment was incredibly charged, and Judi and her husband had a young daughter.

They decided to move to San Diego, near where Judi was born, to live in more relaxed—and warmer—surroundings.

When Judi got to San Diego, she decided to keep teaching her jazz dance classes. Soon she was teaching twenty-five to thirty classes a week. The women loved them. After three or four years, Judi hit a Moment of Truth. It happened when she lost her voice from teaching so many classes. Her doctor said that if she kept teaching twenty-five to thirty classes a week, she was going to do permanent damage to her vocal cords. Judi decided to train five of her best students, so that they could teach classes for her.

> **LESSON LEARNED:** Risk-takers don't
> let ego get in the way of opportunity.

The customers loved the new instructors and told Judi they were so appreciative she had trained them. Judi's ego was a little hurt, but then she realized she had stumbled across a way to expand her operation and reach more women who wanted to move. She realized that if she choreographed the classes, she could teach a lot more instructors.

One day, she sat on her back porch with one of her new instructors, and they talked a bit about money. Judi offered the instructor 70 percent of the proceeds for each class, in exchange for Judi doing the marketing and the choreography. The instructor accepted on the spot. Soon after, when one of her students asked Judi what the class was called, Judi said, "Well, it's jazz dance for fitness and fun." The student said, "That's too long. Nobody will ever remember that name. It should be called Jazzercise because it's part jazz dance and part exercise." Judi liked that idea. One of her other students had a father who was a patent attorney. She registered the name.

One of Judi's student's husbands, Brian Sipe, had gone to San Diego State and became the quarterback of the Cleveland Browns. Judi's student said she wanted to teach the class in Cleveland during the football season.

Jazzercise started spreading like wildfire, its first markets being in Southern California and Ohio. One year later, Judi had over five hundred Jazzercise instructors and she was earning a 30 percent royalty on every class taught.

Judi didn't think about money, but eventually as the operation grew, her accountant and attorney came to see her. They told her, "Judi, you've got to make some changes here because you don't really fit into the niche of being an independent contractor. You're asking a little bit too much of the instructors and you have a little too much control. You have two choices to be legal and not have the IRS come after you. You can either make them employees, or you can make them franchisees."

Judi said she didn't want to make them employees because they all felt like they owned their own business. She wanted them to feel like those classes were their classes because they were. They were teaching their own students and doing the bulk of the work; she was giving them the information and the creative intellectual property to do that. Judi decided to go down the franchise route.

Judi turned out to be a natural marketer and advocate for Jazzercise. She is passionate about movement and the positive role it can play in people's health and lives.

When video camera recorders came out in the late 1970s, Judi recognized that videos would be a business opportunity for Jazzercise. She had her husband, Jack, record their first video of her dancing in their driveway. Today, livestreaming is a significant revenue source for Jazzercise. When her husband mentioned that it would be great for Judi to get on Dinah Shore's television show *Dinah and Friends,* Judi got in her car and drove up to Burbank—and she sat outside the office of one of the production managers until she got a slot on the show.

Jazzercise was the first fitness company to franchise. Then, the first to record a dance fitness album that went gold. Then the first to host charity fundraisers. Along with Domino's Pizza, Jazzercise became one of the hottest franchises of the 1980s. About Domino's, Judi jokes, "It's like we supported each other."

Even as the fitness industry became more competitive, Jazzercise continued to innovate. They've added strength training, kickboxing, and high-intensity interval training classes. Today, the business has over 8,500 franchises in 25 countries, and 32,000 classes are taught each week.

Judi has kept the business very lean for its scale, with only 125 employees. Each year, they host a convention for all their franchisees. Judi still teaches classes, and her daughter, Shanna, helps run the business operation day-to-day as president.

Judi is deeply grateful for her success, humble about her accomplishments, and passionate about how she's helped change the world. "I'm the first person to say it's not just one person," she says. "I have had incredible people around me every single day of my life to help with this. That's the key. Nobody should believe that it's all about them. It isn't. It's about the team you put together and the people you surround yourself with, because they lift you up. They have to buy into your passion. There's no doubt about that. But then you have to be able to bring out the passion they have and use it to enhance what you're doing and give them a place to go at the same time. That's why I think it's been so successful."

At one point, we asked Judi if she's ever raised any external financing. She said no, and that one time she went to a bank for a line of credit but got declined. The loan officer said, "I think you are just an exercise girl and this won't get any bigger." That was about thirty years ago, and the bank closed seven years after Judi met with the loan officer.

To Judi, the explosive growth of Jazzercise has been a natural, organic process. Similarly, to many of the risk-takers we talked to, but perhaps to an extreme, Judi never saw any of her decisions as all that risky.

"People think of me as taking a lot of risks, but I never thought they were risks. To me, it was, *Okay, I'm doing what I love. I'm going to try this. I can do it. It'll be fun. Why not?* Don't think about the negative stuff. Think about what could happen. I think when you're doing your passion, you're able to tune into your gut. It's important to listen to what that voice inside tells you."

LESSON LEARNED: Risk-takers
measure risk internally.

Let's go back to where we started with these Idealists—their deep belief that Mission Transforms Risk (Livewith Six).

Peter Kash is driven by the mission of curing solid-tumor bone cancers. It's why he flies across the world to board meetings, and it is why it excites him to be part of a group of world-class scientists. Zoe Littlepage is driven by doing the right things by her clients, mostly women, who have been wronged by healthcare corporations. It's why she refused to accept deals that would not have been enough for her clients, even when she personally desperately needed settlements. Evan Marwell created The Education Superhighway when he realized schools needed faster internet, and the government couldn't get it done. His sense of mission made all the bureaucratic obstacles surmountable. And Judi Sheppard Missett was driven by the conviction that helping women move their bodies will transform their lives.

Frequently, risk-takers driven by mission find their calling through the events of their lives, which are often traumatic and out of their control. World-changing risk-takers step back from these events and create personal missions in response to them. For Peter Kash, the mission to cure cancer grew out of meeting a bald young girl, before he was old enough to even know what cancer was. Judi's doctor diagnosed her as pigeon-toed before she was two years old. Zoe Littlepage used her senior partners' betrayal to launch a world-changing solo career.

Risk-takers who change the world translate life events into productive missions.

CHAPTER FIVE

Adventurers

No one who met Ed Hillary in his twenties would have guessed that he would become one of the greatest Adventurers of the twentieth century.

Hillary grew up in Auckland, New Zealand. Socially awkward and only an average student, he worked for his father as a beekeeper well into his twenties when he took to climbing mountains as a weekend hobby.

In his early thirties, Ed was hired to support British Himalayan expeditions. His days hauling ninety-pound bags of honey on his father's farm paid off, as Ed had a lean and strong physique even among elite mountain climbers. In 1953, Ed and the Sherpa mountaineer Tenzing Norgay became the first climbers to reach the summit of Mount Everest, the highest point on Earth.

While Hillary's Everest success made him both famous and financially secure, Adventurers tend to have an insatiable appetite for adventure and risk. In 1957, another British team recruited Hillary to establish a re-fueling depot in Antarctica to allow the British to reach the South Pole by land to conduct scientific experiments.

The British leader, Vivian (Bunny) Fuchs, was deliberate and cautious. A year into the expedition in the winter of 1958, Hillary's New Zealand team and the British team were separated, delayed, and facing a second winter in Antarctica.

Hillary took matters into his own hands. Ignoring direct orders from Fuchs and the supervising committees in London, he convinced his teammates to rig four farm tractors to drive the 500 miles to the South Pole. Hillary told his team they should "give it a go," which are the same words he used before summiting Everest. They avoided falling into snow-covered crevasses and safely reached the South Pole.

Hillary was knighted by the Queen soon after his summit, and he and his first wife traveled extensively as he earned a living as a speaker, writer, and celebrity endorser. But he was most entranced by the people of the mountains in Nepal—most of whom could not read or write. They asked Hillary for help building schools. He became fully committed to their cause.

He used his fame to build not only schools, but hospitals and even an airstrip in the high mountain village of Lukla. For the rest of his life, he regularly returned the Himalayas to visit friends. He often said that he was prouder of his aid efforts than his Everest summit.

In early 1975, Hillary completed his first autobiography, in which he concluded, "I look at myself and feel a vast dissatisfaction—there was so much more I could have done. And this is what really counts—not just achieving things . . . but the advantage you have taken of your opportunities and the opportunities you created.

Each of us has to discover his own path—of that, I am sure. Most of all I am thankful for the tasks still left to do—for the adventures still lying ahead."

Adventurers like Hillary exist primarily in what the eminent psychologist Mihaly Csikszentmihalyi has described as the "flow state." Csikszentmihalyi has spent a lifetime observing "flow" experiences, which he describes as follows:

"Flow tends to occur when a person's skills are fully involved in overcoming a challenge that is just about manageable. Optimal experiences usually involve a fine balance between one's ability to act and the available opportunities for action. If the challenges are too high, one gets frustrated, then worried, and eventually anxious. If the challenges are too low relative to one's skills one gets relaxed, then bored . . . But when high challenges are matched with high skills, then the deep involvement that sets flow apart from ordinary life is likely to occur. The climber will feel it when the mountain demands all their strength, the singer when the song demands the full range of their vocal ability . . . and the surgeon when the operation involves new procedures or requires an unexpected variation. A full day is full of anxiety and boredom. Flow experiences provide flashes of intense living against this dull background."[9]

Adventurers gravitate to such a flow state through their risk-taking.

Would it paralyze you to go from a net worth of $100 million to instead owing $100 million in a few months? Would you start two new companies after being diagnosed with incurable cancer? Would you sell your house to fund a new start-up and forget to tell your spouse about it? Would you move your successful business from New Delhi to New York, when you barely knew anyone in New York?

The people that you are about to meet illustrate our first Live-with, the Risk Paradox: taking a risk is the least risky thing you can do, if you want to live a fulfilling life.

Nick Jekogian

"The only thing I was risking was stopping growing.
To me, that was worse than risking it all and losing it all."

Nick Jekogian grew up in the suburbs of Philadelphia. His father was a short-haul truck driver, so he was home every night, and his mom was a homemaker. Nick has a younger brother and sister and was the first in his family to go to college. He started working by mowing lawns when he was twelve and launched a computer programming business at fourteen. Working hard seemed natural to him.

The computer programming business was a failure. Nick partnered with a couple of college seniors from Penn to develop video games, but they didn't sell very many of them. He was the hack programmer for the business venture. Nick leveraged that failure into his first office job, with a real estate company, when he was eighteen and a freshman at Drexel University.

The real estate company was growing fast and had invested thousands of dollars to buy Apple Macintosh computers, which no one knew how to use. Nick was majoring in accounting at Drexel and interviewing for internships with accounting firms when he got the job in the real estate office—real estate intrigued him because, not surprisingly, the real estate company was more entrepreneurial than the accounting firms.

Nick didn't bother to ask how much he was going to get paid when he was hired. His job was to make the Macintosh computers work, and he soon become an indispensable member of the team. They issued him a cell phone, before cell phones were common, so that he could be on call 24/7 in case there was a computer problem.

With Nick's first paycheck he saw that he was making four dollars per hour; twelve dollars per hour less than he could have been making at an accounting firm. It was a trade-off that Nick never regretted. It was there that Nick met some of the real estate developers he still works with to this day.

During his first year—while making Macs work and going to school at Drexel full time—Nick started a new business with a few guys from the office. The business used a large vacuum truck to clean shopping center parking lots at night. Their customers were easy to find since the real estate development company where Nick was working was developing shopping centers.

Nick and his partners cleaned shopping center parking lots for the next four years. This little side business ended up paying for Nick's entire college education. The day he graduated from Drexel, they sold the vacuum truck and shut down the company.

While Nick was still in college, he started buying small walk-up apartment buildings in Philly on his own. It wasn't that he had the cash to do so. When the credit card companies offered applications in exchange for a free bag of peanut M&Ms, Nick filled out all the applications. He was approved for several credit cards, and received many free bags of peanut M&Ms. He bought his first apartment building for $140,000, with $100,000 of bank debt and $40,000 of credit card debt.

We asked Nick how he pulled off getting $100,000 of bank debt with no net worth and a low income as an undergraduate college student. "It helped that the bank was owned by the guy I was working for on the real estate side," he quipped.

Nick's timing was exceptional. In the early nineties, interest rates were low and the real estate market was taking off. Nick bought apartment buildings at below market prices, what are referred to as "distressed assets." He went to graduate business school at Penn and kept buying more apartment buildings whenever he could. When he graduated business school, he accelerated his real estate purchases.

Nick did all this apartment buying through formulas.

"I would refinance the first couple of properties to generate cash and then use that cash to buy the next property. It was the way that pyramids work. It made complete sense to me at the time and still does. I've risked a lot, but I really wasn't risking anything because I had nothing to start with. I was just going out there and doubling down every deal that I bought. We really started ramping this up in 1995, buying these undervalued apartment buildings."

> **LESSON LEARNED:** Risk is only a deterrent
> when one has something to lose.

"We definitely didn't want to hire anyone with real estate experience; we would hire these young people and give them a book of apartments in a city. We'd have them chart out every owner of every apartment building. They would be required to make an offer to every single owner based on this formula that was essentially half the market price. We had a pretty low hit rate, so it was up to these guys to make a lot of offers. Even with a low hit rate, we were able to buy five hundred buildings over a ten-year period."

Nick figured he could train anyone sufficiently smart and entrepreneurial on how to do this, since it just required financial logic and hard work. His first hire was a guy who ran a pizza shop in one of Nick's original employer's shopping centers.

For a while, Nick had another full-time job in New Jersey while he was getting his real estate development company off the ground. He met his partner, the former pizza shop manager, at seven every morning at a diner, and then he would head off to New Jersey to work. They bought twenty-six apartment buildings in that first year.

Nick never felt like he was risking much while working a full-time job and buying twenty-six apartment buildings his first year out of graduate school. He was borrowing money as fast as he could, but he knew the Philly market.

"It's interesting when you look back at it. But when I was in it, it's like I wasn't risking anything. The only risk was if I stopped growing and just became a small-time investor with a couple of apartment buildings. To me, that was worse than risking it all and losing it all."

Making tons of cold calls to property owners using publicly available real estate records, Nick and his partner would seek out older apartment building owners who were hands-off and didn't really understand the value of their properties. Once Nick realized their process worked in one city, he started hiring young college grads, training them on the business model and buying process, and sending them to new cities. They expanded from Philly to Baltimore, and then into Washington, D.C. Soon they put together a more formalized associates program to hire and train more college grads.

After they trained a new college grad, they would buy them a one-way plane ticket to a new city. It took Nick a little more than ten years to expand his business to twenty-five cities throughout the United States and an acquisition team of twenty. The business was buying properties so aggressively that it was always strapped for cash, but this never bothered Nick.

> **LESSON LEARNED:** Big risks are often built on the lessons learned from numerous smaller risks.

By January 2008, about fifteen years after he had started the business, Nick, his wife, and their two young daughters moved to New York City, although the business operations remained in Philadelphia. He had always grown the business by taking on more debt. There was really no other option, other than staying small, for a twenty-five-year-old in 1995 with no real track record or net worth. It wasn't even about negotiating the terms of the debt; it was about getting a seat at the table with the lending banks so he could keep going.

In early 2008 Nick owned $350 million worth of real estate with only $250 million of debt on it—a net worth of $100 million. To Nick, this real estate wasn't about the money—he always lived below his means and didn't need to show off. It was about the game, not the spoils.

Then the stock market crashed in September 2008. Even worse, it crashed because of a real estate bubble. Nick realized that he had always assumed the housing market would keep rising, or at least it wouldn't crash all at once.

"Where I went seriously wrong was always assuming that everybody has to have a place to live. I thought the apartment market would hold up. I wound up having a lot of debt that came due in 2009. I had many projects that hadn't quite finished renovations, but we still had to cover the debt. We had a serious cash flow problem in late 2009 and all those properties, instead of being worth $350 million, were probably worth closer to $175 million. Their value fell literally by half in a matter of twelve months."

By the end of 2008, Nick had gone from a positive net worth of $100 million to a negative net worth of $100 million.

Nick and his wife never talked much about his work. With two young kids there was always plenty else to talk about. His wife grew up in a blue-collar household, like Nick, and she didn't need to live a lavish lifestyle. But suddenly, the banks were coming after Nick. Hard. At his house. Based on his optimism, Nick had personally guaranteed much of the real estate debt. It was just what he needed to do to keep growing the business.

It was not a comfortable time, and it lasted about two years. Nick believed that if he just kept working hard enough, he could muscle his way through his dire financial situation. Throughout 2009 and 2010, he tried to sell his properties to free up cash. But no one was buying.

Nick had always just put his head down and worked his way through things, starting all the way back with his shopping center parking lot cleaning company. But now working harder wasn't working. The meetings with the banks were getting worse and worse. They wanted to take control of all of Nick's real estate holdings.

Finally, based on conversations with young CEOs in a YPO Forum group that Nick had joined, Nick experienced a Moment of Truth. A moment that most likely saved him and his family from total financial ruin.

He realized that the only folks in worse shape than him were the banks pursuing him for cash. The banks held all this debt, but all their creditors were under water. He decided to do the counterintuitive: he started negotiating with the banks to buy back the debt he owed money on, at discounts ranging from 25-90 percent on the dollar.

> **LESSON LEARNED:** Doubling down on
> what got you in trouble doesn't work.

The meetings with the banks weren't pleasant. It took another two years, most of 2011 and 2012, to buy back enough of the bank debt to get back on his feet. And Nick had to sell a lot of property to do it. By the end of 2012, Nick was nowhere near back to where he was in January 2008—in fact he still hasn't gotten back to that point—but he was out from under the daily hassles with the banks. He had about $100 million in property and $75 million in debt, for a net worth of $25 million.

It wasn't easy. Buying back his own debt from banks was not something Nick had ever done before, or hopes he has to do ever again. Lawsuits were delivered to his home on a daily basis, sometimes to his wife when she was alone.

Nick's story is incredible, starting with nothing and taking enormous risks to get to a net worth of $100 million by 2008. What's more incredible is how he has resurrected his business after the real estate market crash.

You could argue that Nick should have seen 2008 coming. Real estate markets are inherently tumultuous and property values weren't going to keep rising forever. Nick was always aware of that, but he didn't prepare for a downturn. Then again, the 2008 market crash was the worst real estate crash since the Great Depression, and Nick wasn't the only one burned by it.

Nick didn't think too much about any of this while it was happening. He is simply not wired to spend much time looking backward. He is wired to work hard, stay in the moment, and look for the next deal. Or, as he puts it, "I'm a deal junkie."

After he went from having $100 million to being at least $100 million in the hole in under a year, Nick kept moving forward, putting one foot in front of the other. Nick mentioned in our discussion that he is an ultra-marathoner. This casual aside might explain more of Nick's personality than anything else. Like his business journey, ultra-marathons involve a lot of putting one foot in front of the other, even in the face of pain, without spending much time contemplating why you are out there in the first place. That's exactly what Nick did from 2008 to 2012.

Nick is a born risk-taker and Adventurer. He says, "If I didn't take those risks, where would I be? I'd be in a decent-sized house, with two kids and a dog and everything taken care of, but that's all it would be. To me, it was a much bigger risk to live that type of lifestyle, than to do what I do for a living."

This life view was hugely beneficial in 2008, because he had no need to look back with regret. Nick has always known he is living the life that he has consciously chosen.

Nick's motivation is more about adventure and growth than money. He openly admits that he doesn't know what he would do with a lot more money if he had it. He values, even relishes, the obstacles that he finds in front of him. He used the aftermath of the 2008 crash to pause and reflect. "After I lost it all, I started thinking . . . I started seeing the world differently. I came to the realization that in our lives we have different decades where we do different things. Our first couple of decades, it's all about us. Then it's working for other people to help build skills and make money, and then it's raising kids and how we work or assist the industry we're in. I think I'm rolling into the part now where my purpose will be for a fulfilled life. It will be more than just for me and my family, and it will be much more of a global focus. Now I'm focused on straightening out my financial life so that I can leverage that into a more global focus as I turn fifty."

Most risk-takers, but not all, are reluctant to see their children take the risks that they did. But Nick doesn't see it that way. When thinking about his children's risk-taking, what he says embodies the essence of the Adventurers' view of risk-taking:

"I'd say yes, do it. I would be worried if they didn't. My kids are going to college in a couple of years. Then in five, six years, they're going to have that opportunity to take two types of jobs, right? They'll have the opportunity to go work for Google or Microsoft, make $250,000 a year, and that will be their life. Or there'll be some cool start-ups out there where they don't make half of that money but get the rest in stock. It will either be a phenomenal success or they'll wind up with nothing. I would always tell them to go take the start-up, get the experience, and see what happens. Live the life. Take risks. I'm a big believer in that, if you don't take risks, you don't really live, and that's the biggest risk you ever really take in your life."

Phil Brabbs

"My dad said something that is always haunting me.
'Phil, if you find a job you love, you'll never call it work.'"

Nobody has faced more obstacles than Phil Brabbs. He grew up in Midland, Michigan, where his father worked at Dow Chemical, like nearly everyone else in town. But he wasn't a chemist. He was a blue-collar worker, a construction manager, and he had a side hustle of building houses. Phil had a strong mother and four older sisters who tried to push him around. He always believed that, if given a chance, he could outwork anyone. To this day, that's his approach to success.

Phil learned in Midland that he was good at two things: math and athletics. He went to the University of Michigan in the late 1990s to study engineering and play football. He walked onto the football team and was a few years behind a teammate named Tom Brady. Phil excelled in high school football, where he was a star cornerback and wide receiver, but at Michigan his only shot to make the team was as a kicker. He earned a football scholarship and kicked the game-winning field goal against Illinois in August 2002. Later that year, he suffered an injury and realized he needed to let go of football and get a job in engineering.

Fortunately, Phil loved technology. He got married right after college, found a tech consulting job with Accenture, and moved to Charlotte. While there, Phil started suffering from a mysterious health issue. No one could figure out what was wrong. Phil was an extremely fit and healthy guy in his mid-twenties who ran marathons in his spare time. It turned out he was having blood clots, which caused a pulmonary embolism.

Phil's health and the arrival of their first child, a son, resulted in Phil and his wife rethinking where to live. They decided to move back to Michigan to be closer to their families. By then, Phil had caught the entrepreneurial bug and started building websites as a side business. Accenture demanded that he travel more than he wanted to with a young family, so he took a job with a healthcare data company in Ann Arbor, less than a mile from his house. Phil was now working in the product management group that one of us, Doug, was leading.

Phil and his wife were thrilled to be back in Ann Arbor. Everything was going well . . . with one exception. The blood clots kept coming back. Phil's natural inclination was to ignore his health issues, but a woman in his church had started working for a great primary care doctor in Ann Arbor, and she convinced Phil to go see that doctor. The primary care doctor ran some blood tests and noticed some results that were seriously out of whack; she referred Phil to an oncologist. Phil didn't even know what an oncologist did.

The oncologist ordered a bone marrow biopsy. The results were not good. Phil was diagnosed with multiple myeloma on August 8, 2008, just after he'd turned twenty eight years old. Multiple myeloma is an incurable blood cancer, although many people who are diagnosed with it live for a long time. At the time of his diagnosis, Phil and his wife had just had their second child.

Phil didn't feel sick, he was training for another marathon when he was diagnosed. He had a wife who didn't have a college degree and two young kids. He did what he had always done and plowed ahead and went back to work. The oncologist couldn't tell how bad the cancer was, so he needed to regularly monitor his bloodwork. Meanwhile, his wife did a lot of internet research. Together, Phil and his wife created a blog called *MM for Dummies*, which became quite popular in the multiple myeloma patient community.

Phil was tracking his bloodwork in a spreadsheet and the numbers were getting worse. He could see the cancer growing, and it was all becoming more real. He and his wife decided to visit the University of Arkansas in Little Rock to get a second opinion. The trip confirmed their fears. The specialists found the cancer had quickly tripled in size. They wanted him to stay in Little Rock for up to nine months and receive two bone marrow transplants, which would, in the memorable words of the oncologist there, "put you as close to death as we can get you." There was a chance to eradicate the cancer, but it was going to be a long road.

Phil and his wife returned to Ann Arbor and found an oncologist there who could perform a similar protocol. In Phil's mind, the decision to stay in Ann Arbor was clear: "The hospital here is two miles from my house. I have two young kids. I thought, *If I'm going to die in this process, I don't want to die in Little Rock. No, I'm going to be here. I'm going to be with them. I'm going to be with my wife. I'm going to live with my family. I'm going to live in my community.* I really felt fortunate to meet that oncologist. So, I got treatment here in Ann Arbor. I think at that point, the whole experience started to shift within me."

The reality of Phil's multiple myeloma diagnosis was not good. There was only a one-in-three chance of surviving more than five years. Phil was in excellent shape physically and still only in his twenties, so he gave himself a fifty-fifty chance of surviving five years. Still, after his trip to Arkansas, he had a new perspective. "It put me in this state of I'm not going to live a life that's not driven by purpose. I'm not going to work at a place that I don't believe in, want to be part of, and that I'm not passionate about. I'm not going to set goals that aren't going to support my family whether I'm here or not."

People who don't take much risk perpetuate a myth that people should wait for the "right moment" to take risks. For risk-takers, a precipitating life event often changes their life direction to align with a purpose. Sometimes this is an adverse life event, like being diagnosed with cancer. In several ways, Phil's job in Ann Arbor fit his challenging life circumstances well. The office was a mile from his house, and he didn't have to travel. The company had great health insurance and would be flexible and supportive when he needed to take long-term disability leave. He knew there would be a job for him there when he could work full-time again.

The problem was, there was nothing in the job that fulfilled Phil's life purpose. Phil felt like he was punching the clock in a soulless place. Everything changed when he realized he might not have much time left. His cancer diagnosis helped Phil see life and business in starker terms. There was no reason to mince words.

"My desire was to help other people unleash their deepest desires and passion and purpose in life. I had an inkling that I'd be like a life coach in a very simple sense. I wanted to help other individuals try that thing in them that's uniquely them and help them activate it. That's what I wanted. All the rhetoric from the healthcare business felt like puffery. I saw the pattern. It had nothing to do with me, and really frustrated me. If that's what business is about, screw it. I wasn't being true to myself."

Just like his dad, Phil always had a side hustle. When the reality of his cancer diagnosis hit him, he did what many would consider inadvisable and even reckless: he poured energy into his side hustle, even while he kept his day job. When Phil's direct boss came to Doug, explaining Phil's illness, Doug approved the game plan of having Phil work from home as much as possible—but he didn't know about all the side hustles until we interviewed Phil for this book!

Phil's first side hustle was a customer relationship management (CRM) software product for college coaches needing to keep track of recruiting prospects. His father-in-law was a college volleyball coach at the time. Phil had gained experience in implementing CRM systems back at Accenture, so he knew the territory. He and a few others started building the CRM system for big schools like Michigan, Michigan State, and Northwestern. Between 2008 and 2010—after Phil's diagnosis—they built a business with thirty paying customers.

Phil was working full-time at his day job and nights and early mornings in the CRM business. They couldn't find a technical co-founder, so they outsourced the software development to India. Phil was the product guy in the small start-up, running agile product development sprints at five in the morning with the India team.

There was nothing easy about Phil's life. The stock market crashed in 2008, and the CRM business wasn't yet profitable. Phil pulled the $8,000 or so that he had in his 401(k) out so that he could invest it all in the CRM business. He felt he was doing what he was meant to do professionally, building a tech start-up as a legacy to support his family.

Believe it or not, during this time Phil had more than his cancer diagnosis and his CRM side hustle to deal with. The doctors in Arkansas told Phil and his wife that he might become sterile as a result of the bone marrow transplants. They had two kids whom they loved deeply, and they decided they wanted a third. They had six weeks to get pregnant with a third child before the bone marrow transplants.

Phil's third child was born in April 2010. Within three months he underwent two bone marrow transplants, which, as the oncologist had predicted, made him very ill. He finally went on disability at his day job and, when the long-term disability kicked in, he made only 60 percent of his salary.

Around this time, Phil met an experienced mentor who advised him to raise investment money for his side-hustle-CRM software company. He and his partners raised $450,000 in angel funding, which enabled them to bring in a technical co-founder and start building software in the United States. Phil couldn't quit his day job though, because he needed the health insurance. And the investment money, like all investment money, came with strings attached.

Phil and his CRM team used the investment money for product development and sales. Phil was in charge of sales, but he was sick and couldn't leave his day job. He hired a salesperson, who quickly took the customer base from thirty to three hundred. With the customers and with the investors came more stress. The business was up to $250,000 per year in revenue, but still wasn't profitable. And there was an argument building between Phil and two of his partners about the product. The partners were more technical than Phil and wanted to re-build the whole product. Phil didn't want to make that investment. They started to run out of money. Now, the angel investors were in the power position, and they started to squeeze Phil and the management team.

In January 2012 it all crashed.

LESSON LEARNED: You can't ignore your own health for long, no matter what else is going on professionally.

Phil was working two jobs, raising three kids, on chemo, recovering from the bone marrow transplants, and drinking coffee like a madman. His body gave out, and he ended up back in the University of Michigan hospital. He had almost worked himself to death.

The next two weeks in the hospital were harrowing. Phil wasn't sure he was going to make it out. When he did, he reflected on how he had ended up in such bad shape, and decided he had to re-focus on his health and his family. It was right then the angel investors called in their loan to the start-up and took control of the business. Via email. Phil still can't believe the investors did this when the company was growing and on a path to success. He was kicked out of his own business with a minority equity share, which has never paid out.

Yet Phil still had the start-up bug, and one of his best friends from the CRM company was now working on a new start-up called Torrent Consulting. Phil wasn't ready to leave his day job, so he started out advising his friend. They were working off a business plan Phil built years ago that focused not just on CRM but also on building a company that would allow employees to achieve their full potential. There was tremendous focus on creating the right culture.

The more Phil advised his friend, the more passionate he became. Phil is an all-in or all-out guy, and in late 2012 he experienced a Moment of Truth. He realized that he either had to commit to the new start-up, or he couldn't be involved.

On January 7, 2013, Phil resigned from his full-time day job. His cancer lab tests were looking better, and he had a young, growing family. He had to make the leap for his own sanity. His co-founder and many of the first customers were in Charlotte, which meant more travel.

"In the early years of Torrent, it was like family. The three people I was working with were some of my closest friends. I was able to support and serve them. It was great. It was interesting though, because back then we couldn't see more than two days ahead of ourselves. Our vision went about two days. Things were changing that fast."

Phil had never felt such a sense of purpose before. "My dad said something that always haunted me. He said, 'Phil, if you find a job you love, you'll never call it work.' So, I always felt I needed to find a job where I had purpose and passion, because that way I'd know that's where I needed to be. For ten years, I had not found it. Yet, every day at Torrent, every day that I was there, I loved it. Sure, there were ugly days. There were depressing days. There were joyous days. But I wouldn't trade any of those days with the previous ten years."

Phil didn't think of the risk of leaving his stable day job for a start-up as a financial concern, though he gave up his health insurance at a time most would consider crazy. But that didn't bother him either. He had confidence that he would find a way, another path, if Torrent didn't work out. Phil was more worried about the opposite risk. What would he lose by staying at his job? We call this risk the Risk Avoidance Fallacy—underestimating the risks of just staying where you are.

> **KEY CONCEPT—RISK AVOIDANCE FALLACY:**
> Believing you can avoid risk by staying in your current situation because it will not change. Everything changes.

If he stayed, Phil would lose the chance to create the workplace culture he'd always dreamed of. He would lose the chance to be true to himself, which he committed to as he persevered through life-threatening bone marrow transplants. After that, who could blame him for taking risks to live a life true to himself?

Torrent Consulting grew into a successful firm with four US offices, one international office, and many customers. It happened without any external investors. Phil has a rarified ability to work backward from a vision and bend reality to achieve it.

Recently, Phil realized he had lost his balance again. Torrent consumed too much of his physical and mental capacity. Everything else—his family life, his exercise program, his spiritual life—was suffering. Phil realized that he is good at being "all in," good at being addicted to adventure, but not so good at juggling several competing priorities. He decided to phase himself out of Torrent, and he now works at the University of Michigan Business School, where he is the managing director of a new center called Value Chain Innovation. He teaches operations management courses, which bring together three areas where he has deep experience: technology, entrepreneurship, and innovation.

Phil's story illuminates our first Risk Livewith: that taking a risk is personal, but it needs to occur in the context of your whole life. Several times, despite his best intentions, Phil had to pull back on the risk he was taking to get his life—and health—back in balance.

Michael Saltman

"I have a real independent streak as a result of that tragic event in my life, but it gave me the strength to survive."

Michael Saltman was born in Flint, Michigan, in 1942. He was very close to his father, who took him along on business trips, to baseball games, and on fishing trips. On January 3, 1957, his father died of a heart attack. Michael was fourteen years old. He says even today, "I still haven't fully recovered from his death."

After his father's death, Michael's mom went back to school to do graduate work at the University of Michigan. This seems to be the time when Michael became an Adventurer. "I was left to pretty much raise myself, and that's what I did. I have a real independent streak as a result of that tragic event in my life, but it gave me the strength to survive and thrive over many years of making decisions for myself."

Michael has always loved to travel. When he graduated from Michigan State University, he drove to LA to work for a public relations firm. A few months after he moved to California, his mom called him and asked him, "When are you going to law school? If you don't go now, you may never go." Michael thought about that and decided she was right. He came back, showed up at the admissions office of Wayne State Law School in Detroit, and the dean happened to be there. When he showed the Dean his transcripts and recommendations, he was admitted on the spot.

An influential law school professor helped Michael gain a scholarship in his third year and suggested that he attend graduate school in the UK or Europe after getting his law degree and being admitted to the bar. This was a Moment of Truth. Michael could have easily stayed in Detroit and worked for General Motors, but his heart and wanderlust told him to move to London.

However, after six months at the University College, London, he grew disenchanted with classes and dropped out. To clear his head he went for a holiday in Majorca. Before he left, he purchased an ad in the *International Herald Tribune* which read, "Young lawyer seeks interesting international challenge."

When Michael returned from Majorca, he had several offers for interviews in his post office box.

One of those offers was with an insurance company called International Life. This turned out to be the first in a series of international assignments, which enabled Michael to travel all over the world and live in London, Geneva, and Munich. He met his wife, Sonja, an Austrian, while living in London, and they've been married over forty-five years. He was living in Munich during the 1972 Olympics when most of the Israeli team was taken hostage and killed.

When the oil crisis hit in 1974, Michael's European business opportunities dried up. Fortunately, he had a friend in Geneva whose father owned properties in Las Vegas. The friend asked him to move to Las Vegas to help develop the properties.

Like many Adventurers, Michael makes decisions based on informed intuition. He had only driven through it a few times, but he had a sense that Las Vegas, then a town of only 260,000 people, could become a boomtown. In another Moment of Truth, Michael and Sonja sold everything they had in Munich and moved sight unseen to Vegas.

LESSON LEARNED: Adventurers in particular often rely on informed intuition for big, risky decisions.

In Vegas, Michael envisioned his own real estate development firm, following his father's dream. Michael partnered with a well-known mechanical contractor in Las Vegas to buy property across from the University of Nevada, Las Vegas, for $412,500, with only a $10,000 down payment. (Michael remembers the exact purchase prices of all the properties he has bought over the years.)

Michael wanted to build a 125-unit apartment complex on the property, but he needed another loan. New York Life refused because much of the infrastructure investment money in Las Vegas then came from the Teamsters Union, which was viewed as mob-connected. "The town is red-lined, son, and we can't help you." Every Monday morning for the next three months Michael parked himself on the doorstep of the New York Life office in LA. He finally got the loan. He didn't have much cash so his partner put up 90 percent of the equity in the deal. This was Michael's start.

For the next nineteen years, from 1975 to 1995, Michael had an incredible run as a developer in Las Vegas. He and his partner sold the apartment complex at a healthy profit. Next they bought a vacant 160-acre lot in the desert outside Las Vegas for $5,000 an acre, and sold it to a home-building company for $21,000 an acre just thirteen months later. From the profits they built a series of apartments and strip malls.

Of course, not everything in real estate development goes smoothly. Inflation and interest rates rose dramatically in the late 1970s. One of their construction loans had a variable interest rate, and one day in 1979 the bank called and raised their interest rate from 9 percent to 21 percent. They almost ran out of cash but managed to beg and borrow, but not steal, to stay afloat.

Michael began developing shopping centers with grocery stores as anchor tenants. In 1986, he got into the grocery store business by accident. In one of his shopping centers in Las Vegas, the anchor tenant was a stripped-down, low-price grocery store. As they competed the project, the board chair of the grocery store was diagnosed with cancer. The family that owned the grocery store pulled out of the deal.

It was another Moment of Truth. Knowing that he needed the anchor tenant, Michael raised $500,000 to become an equity partner with the grocer. The store worked out well, and Michael and the family expanded the unusual concept for the business, called Food4Less, building shopping centers with the grocery store as the anchor throughout Nevada and Utah.

His success with the grocery caught the eye of another major family that owned similar grocery stores in Southern California. They approached Michael and built a relationship with him. Eventually, the Southern California family—with Michael as a partner—ended up buying out the original family business from the Vegas shopping mall. They continued to buy small grocery store chains throughout the Western United States.

Michael didn't know when he originally raised $500,000 to save a grocery store tenant how well his investment would work out. After eight years, the entire chain was sold to a national grocery store behemoth in which Michael became an equity partner.

After surviving and thriving in the many ups and downs of real estate development, Michael began selling properties in the mid-2000s. By then he was in his early sixties and real estate values were high.

He started a mortgage company in Las Vegas to lend money to developers, thinking that debts secured by real estate were never going to fail. Like Nick, he didn't see the real estate crash of 2008 coming.

> **LESSON LEARNED:** Adventurers don't have a finish line indicating when they are done taking risks.

He survived because his sizable office real estate portfolio in Nevada, Utah, and California somewhat insulated him from the crash. But he had to sell off many of his properties and foreclose on many homes in Las Vegas to get through the crisis.

Michael is now in his seventies. "My tavern business is doing well again, our Southern California properties are up and operating, and I'm a university trustee at UNLV. My wife and I are the founders of the Saltman Center for Conflict Resolution at the law school, which is always ranked as one of the top ten conflict resolution programs in the country. I'm launching a new venture in Israel right now with a partner, bringing technology to Nevada from Israel. I'm always looking for development opportunities."

Michael's sense of humor and adventure, and indeed his sense of exploration and wonder, has never left him. Toward the end of our discussion, he quoted a song from the movie, *The Mule*: "Don't let the old man in." Michael is not letting the old man in.

Andrew White

"She didn't know I put the house on the market
until she saw the sign in the yard."

Alan met Andrew White in Houston when he joined YPO, a leadership community for young chief executives, and he joined Andrew's forum group. Alan quickly realized that Andrew was direct and humble, yet confident in his own abilities. He seemed to have a huge appetite for risk-taking.

Andrew's father was in state politics in Texas, starting when Andrew was six months old. His dad made it all the way to being governor of Texas—a fact that Andrew never mentioned to Alan when they first met—before losing an election when Andrew was fourteen. From an early age, Andrew was more interested in business than politics. He remembers taking the *Wall Street Journal* from the governor's mansion with him to read in junior high school. When his father lost his re-election bid, the family moved from Austin to Houston and his dad returned to his law practice.

Even though Andrew's dad was governor, the family never had a lot of money. Andrew always knew he needed to make his own money to buy the stuff he wanted as a kid. He ran a lemonade stand until he could afford the bike he wanted. His grandmother taught him to make peanut brittle so that he could sell it at his junior high.

Andrew's parents were very busy. There were never big problems between them, but they weren't very involved with his life. His dad didn't have that much wealth and was not interested in business, but he had many successful friends. Andrew would try to hang out with his dad's business friends even when he was still in high school. One of them was a stockbroker at Kidder Peabody. When Andrew asked the guy for advice on buying stocks, he told Andrew to just look at the companies whose stock had gone down that day in the *Wall Street Journal*, and buy those stocks the next day, because that's where he would find value. The stockbroker was probably just trying to get Andrew to go away, but Andrew took his advice. Pretty soon, he had built up a small stock portfolio.

Andrew went to the University of Virginia as a religious studies major, but he took many courses in accounting and finance. He graduated in three years. It was during his second year that Andrew discovered investment banking. All the big New York firms were hiring undergrads from UVA, and some of the banks liked to take liberal arts majors, like Andrew, and train them on investment banking. It was exactly what Andrew wanted to do: analyze companies, structure financial deals, and live in New York. After college, he took the first job offer that he got from a bulge bracket investment bank, Credit Suisse, and moved to New York.

Andrew knew he wouldn't always be the smartest guy in the room, but he had a positive attitude and believed he could outwork anyone. After a few years, Andrew realized that while his time in

New York was great professional experience, it was a terrible personal experience. He had no life outside of work. He could make a lot of money in New York, but he hated the lifestyle.

Andrew's dad was on the board of a small industrial services company in Houston that was growing by making acquisitions. Andrew wanted to be "a bigger fish in a smaller pond" and applied to be their business development manager. He only stayed about eighteen months, but this was his first step toward the life he wanted.

For the next six years, Andrew got involved with several small business opportunities in Dallas and Houston. None of them took off, but he learned firsthand how to structure transactions and deal with investors.

> **LESSON LEARNED:** Many young risk-takers learn from early fast failures.

First, Andrew and the COO from the small industrial services company secured investors to buy the shell of an empty public company. They acquired an industrial coatings business in Chicago, but the more successful they were, the more the investors exerted control. Finally, the investors sold the business. Andrew didn't have much equity and made very little.

By then, it was the late 1990s, and the height of the dot-com boom. Andrew became a member of the founding team of an online wholesale club called Market City USA, which innovated an online shopping cart like you find on Amazon today. Andrew put all of his money ($35,000) into the business. He was twenty-five years old. Then the dot-com bubble burst, and the business failed.

Andrew's and all of his investors' money disappeared.

Andrew, being an Adventurer, didn't look back. He still had confidence he would find a way to make something work. As he was looking for his next adventure, he met his future wife. At their wedding, he told everyone he was "self-unemployed."

Next, Andrew became CFO of a home restoration business. It was a small company that had gone public and their stock was trading on the American Stock Exchange. He was in his early thirties, and it was 2005; the housing market was still good. By now, Andrew had two kids with another on the way. He and his wife had put their $100,000 savings into a nice house in West U, close to Rice University and one of the trendier places to live in Houston. Andrew was making a good salary, but he was traveling all over the place to help the company make more acquisitions.

It was starting to remind him too much of his New York banking experience.

Andrew's company evaluated a home warranty business in California. They passed on the deal, but Andrew got to know the CEO pretty well. Andrew didn't understand the ins and outs of the home warranty business, but what he did understand, he liked. With the CEO's encouragement, he decided to create a similar business in Texas, from scratch.

Andrew told his wife, "Well, I could always work at Frito Lay in marketing if this doesn't work out." That was his tongue-in-cheek plan B. He didn't want to work at Frito Lay, nor had they ever offered him a job.

"I was thinking that all I needed to do was create a business that made enough money that I could replicate or beat the Frito Lay salary. If I could pull that off, then I could control my schedule and be my own boss and enjoy the benefits of that. So, I didn't have this huge hurdle that I had to get over. I knew I needed to make $100,000–$200,000, and if I could make that, then I'd be in great shape.

"I do think it takes a lot of self-confidence, maybe too much self-confidence, to start a business from scratch. I mean, looking back on it, when you're thirty-two, you're at a certain stage in life. My kids were still young. I didn't have the overhead that comes with time and families. I knew that was going to change, and I knew that if I was going to do this, now was the time. And failing with kids in high school looks different than failing with kids in preschool. It just does. And so, I knew this was the time I had to get it done."

> **LESSON LEARNED:** Risk tastes different with age.

"I think that if I'd known all the risks, I wouldn't have done it. I mean, you can argue that about any start-up. You're blind to the reality that's against you. If you really were 'smart' and understood all those risks, you'd be an idiot for doing it. So, there's a certain amount of self-confidence that blinds you and you just believe in yourself.

"If it works, you're a hero. If it doesn't work, then nobody wants to interview you. They don't write books about the people who fail. And what is failure? Failure is losing all your money, for one. But failure is also having a business where you've worked like crazy, and you make $42,000 a year—when you could be working at Frito Lay and making $82,000—and then you're really stuck because you can't get away."

Andrew started his own home warranty business in Houston

from scratch, calling it Allied Home Warranty. He needed $100,000 in cash, and the only way he could figure out how to get that was by selling his house.

His wife swears to this day that she only found out the house was for sale when she came home from running errands and saw the *For Sale* sign in the yard. That's when Andrew explained to his wife what he was up to with Allied Home Warranty.

Andrew doesn't remember it exactly that way, but admits his wife could be right, "I literally just thought to myself: *We've got to sell the house to start the business.* And I put the house on the market before she even knew about it. I mean, she says that she didn't know about it at all until she saw the sign in the yard. And I think to myself, *Surely, I must have mentioned something to her ahead of time?* Maybe I didn't. It's possible."

LESSON LEARNED: Adventurers exhibit intense focus.

The next place Andrew, his wife, and three kids lived was a small, dumpy apartment rental pretty far from West U. One day they were watching TV as it rained outside, when a rat raced across the carpet. Andrew and his wife have a good marriage, but she wasn't happy about the rat.

Andrew had a ready-fire-aim mentality in those early days. First, he rented a small office in a building down the street from their apartment. It was more of a supply closet than an office. He had folding tables, a phone, and internet access. Next, he finalized his service contract and got approval from the state—both milestones in the home warranty business.

Andrew was doing everything himself and realized he needed

help. He made a brochure and stuck it in a few real estate offices. Within a few days he got a phone call from a woman who was a top salesperson at a large competitor. She was frustrated with her current job and wanted to meet for lunch. She complained how her company was treating its customers poorly. He hired her right after the lunch, and in thirty days sold seventy-five new contracts, each paying $350 per month. That was when it hit Andrew that he had a real business, along with the responsibility of paying employees and serving customers.

Allied Home Warranty grew quickly in 2005 and 2006. Soon annual revenue was up to $600,000 with only five employees. He expanded from Houston to San Antonio, delicately managing cash reserves to comply with minimums required in the home warranty business.

As he expanded into Dallas, Andrew met an investor interested in his business. Andrew needed cash to enable growth, but he was burned badly before by losing control of the business. The investor put in $500,000 for 40 percent of the business.

About eighteen months in, Andrew saw an opportunity to branch out into the home repair business. He realized if they could do their own home repair, their home warranty contracts would be more profitable. Andrew's investors didn't want him to lose focus on the home warranty business. Eventually they allowed him to start the second business, but they didn't invest any money in it.

Andrew created a new home repair business called Lone Star, and he was the sole owner. It took three years, but Lone Star became profitable. Andrew introduced technology innovations like technicians using iPads at home sites to provide real-time information on repair status and cost.

Andrew was diligent about continual improvement at both Allied and Lone Star. He wasn't making much money himself—he had negotiated a salary of $120,000 at Allied—but both businesses were lucrative and growing. Andrew was quick to introduce innovations that were harder for his bigger competitors to roll out.

When the housing market crisis hit in 2008, the home warranty business flattened, and cash was tight; Andrew was scrambling to meet his reserve requirements. Andrew went to his investors, with whom he had a sometimes-problematic relationship, and asked them if he should try to sell the business on the downside. To their credit, they said no. Instead, they invested another $500,000 and Andrew kept control of the business with a 52 percent share. The investors came through during the worst possible market conditions.

Then came Andrew's big break. A competitor asked Andrew if he did any business with utilities. He said no, but he started wondering if he should. A few weeks later he was pushing his daughter on a swing set at the local church playground when he met Roger, who was pushing his own daughter next to him. They started talking about what they did for a living. It turned out Roger worked at NRG Reliant, the large electric utility company in Houston. Andrew asked Roger to make some introductions at Reliant, and he was more than happy to do so.

Roger's contact at Reliant was working on a request for proposal (RFP) to outsource a new program to protect customer homes from electrical surges. Andrew worked the RFP hard for six months. He eventually lost the deal, but instead of getting upset, he stayed in touch with his contacts at Reliant.

A month later, Reliant called Andrew—they hadn't yet reached an agreement with the winning bidder on the RFP and were getting

frustrated with the negotiation. They offered Andrew a deal—
Reliant would do the billing and collection, and Allied would do
the delivery on the surge protection program, with a fifty-fifty
revenue split. Andrew took the deal on the spot. He knew this
was his big break.

LESSON LEARNED: Successful risk-takers realize
their big breaks when they happen to them.

The surge protection program was extremely profitable for both
Reliant and Allied.

"NRG Reliant, after much thought, decided they wanted to buy
us. Their reasons for buying us were interesting, because it had
nothing to do with the business that we'd created for them. It had
nothing to do with strategically aligning with a home service pro-
vider so they could have Reliant trucks driving around. It had
nothing to do with the money we were making for them. The only
reason they bought us was because the CEO of NRG wanted to
do solar. Even though we had never done that before, maybe we
could start selling solar through our trucks. That's why they spent
$65 million on this deal, because he thought they might be able to
sell solar from our trucks. That was not the reason I would have
bought the business."

Andrew's business, which he had started by selling his house and
renting an office supply closet, was bought for $65 million, and
he had a 52 percent ownership stake. He wanted to make enough
money to live his own life and support his kids' modest hobbies,
and now he had done far better than that.

Andrew isn't sure that he would have tried to create the business if he had known how long the odds of success were, but he's glad that he did.

"I don't believe in luck because I can't just say I got lucky," he says. "What is luck? I don't know. I believe in a world that has a creator. If there's a creator in the world, then there is no such thing as luck. So, I don't believe in luck.

"But I think about all the things that happened that were fortuitous in the sense of timing. I started the business right before the massive housing growth. A rising tide lifts all boats. The industry was going gangbusters. I was in Texas, an even better spot. The woman who saw my brochure, that was in literally two offices in the entire city. She set off this massive sales opportunity; she was the right person at the right time. And then, I'm pushing my daughter on a swing and talking to a guy who happened to follow up on a request and put me in touch with the guy who happens to be a great cheerleader within the organization. And then, they decide they want to buy my business."

Andrew's experience illustrates all of the Risk Livewiths. Because he could always get a job at Frito Lay, he felt he had nothing to lose. In his mind what he did wasn't that risky (The Risk Paradox). Although Andrew is a "numbers guy," he understands the role of emotions in making decisions—when NRG Reliant came back to him with a fifty-fifty revenue split on the surge protection program, he took the deal on the spot (Livewith Two: Head and Heart). Andrew wasn't afraid to put his house up for sale to fund his business, although we would advise to tell your spouse about that first (Livewith Three: Life *Is* Risk). Andrew wasn't paralyzed by his early business failures and just kept going (Livewith Four: Risk Never Fails to Teach). He says now that, had he known what he knows now, he wouldn't have taken some of the risks he did, but he also recognizes he was different when he was younger (Livewith Five: Risk Tastes Different with Age). Finally, Andrew clearly had a burning desire to succeed (Livewith Six: Mission Transforms Risk); he values money, mostly for the life freedom that it can provide.

Adventurers bring to real life three major conclusions from our research:

- Risk-takers think more about the downsides of *not* taking the risk, rather than the potential downsides of taking the risk. To Nick, nothing could be worse than a life without risk. Phil ultimately wasn't willing to tolerate working at places which were unaligned with the goal of enabling everyone to fulfill their potential. And Andrew was okay with just about anything other than a boring job at Frito Lay.

- Risk is about what we choose during those Moments of Truth, those turning points in our lives. In Andrew's Moment of Truth, he took the NRG Reliant deal without running the numbers. In Phil's, he quit his day job despite his cancer diagnosis.

- Risk is about dealing with obstacles without getting stuck. Nick was on a roll until the biggest housing market crash in seventy-plus years; Michael got into the grocery business when one of his key tenants got cancer; Phil overcame life-threatening health challenges and struggled with balancing his family life with his professional ambitions; and Andrew had to sell his house to fund his new business—but they all faced their obstacles head-on and with a belief that they would find a way through. Adventurers experience plenty of obstacles and failures, but they process these events differently than most others. They see them largely as learning opportunities and part of the flow of life.

All Adventurer interviewees got comfortable with obstacles and mistakes. When we interviewed Brian Scudamore, founder and CEO of 1-800-Got-Junk, a hugely successful company, he emphasized, "Every failure I've had—and there have been some that didn't seem at the time like a 'good failure'—is just a stepping-stone to a better place. You learn from your mistakes." Brian even co-authored a book titled *WTF?! Willing to Fail: How Failure Can Be Your Key to Success.*

Adventurers view risk-taking and living as synonymous. When they do experience setbacks, they don't let themselves stay down for long. They live in the present, and they don't spend time looking back with regret.

There is much to learn from Adventurers. They are joyful warriors, navigating an often-complicated world.

CHAPTER SIX

Liberators

Risk-takers aren't just driven by what they want to accomplish. They are also driven by independence. Those who desire independence don't want to work for a large company, with layers of management, rules, and processes. They don't want to be "just a number" or a cog in the wheel of life. They don't want someone else to tell them what to do.

Ken Burns is a world-renowned documentary filmmaker. Ken is fiercely independent, obsessive about maintaining creative control—a classic Liberator. Documentaries are not a lucrative niche; most of his films are shown on the Public Broadcasting System.

Ken Burns risks his time, and the time of those he works with, rather than his money, to support his fierce independence.

The seeds of Ken's free-agent life were planted early. His parents were academics and moved frequently before settling in Ann Arbor, Michigan. His mother was diagnosed with breast cancer when Ken was three years old and died when he was eleven. Ken's father-in-law, a psychologist, once told him that his "whole work was an attempt to make people long gone come back alive." It's an insight that Ken believes traces back to his mother's early death.

Ken has structured his entire career, indeed his life, to maintain his independence. In his mid-twenties he moved from New York to rural Walpole, New Hampshire, so that—in the tradition of many young free agents—he could lower his cost of living.

Ken's passion for his work, as expressed in many interviews, is visceral. His craft is storytelling, and he has said that for each of his documentaries, he collects forty to fifty times the material that actually ends up in the film. Whether this is efficient or wise, he answers to no one about this practice.

Now in his late sixties, Ken is hardly done taking risks. He has already announced documentaries on Muhammad Ali (2021), Benjamin Franklin (2022), the Holocaust (2023), the American Buffalo (2024), Leonardo da Vinci (2025), the American Revolution (2025), and LBJ and the Great Society (2027). These are topics of his passions, his interests, and are, as a true Liberator, pursued on his terms.

Above all, risk-takers motivated by independence want to own their own life. And they are willing to make 180-degree turns to achieve this. They are less driven by the specific idea that they are pursuing than the desire to own their life. They will quickly change course if something isn't working, which is necessary in a messy world where many ideas don't work out.

Working for a large company no longer offers all the employment security and benefits that it used to. In 2001, Daniel H. Pink heralded the beginning of a new century with his book *Free Agent Nation*.[10] Pink describes the shift to free agent work as a result of four dynamics:

- "The social contract of work—in which employers traded loyalty for security—crumbled."

- "Individuals needed a large company less, because the means of production—that is, the tools necessary to create wealth—went from expensive, huge, and difficult for one person to operate to cheap."

- "Widespread, long-term prosperity allowed people to think of work as a way to not only make money, but also to make meaning."

- "The half-life of organizations began shrinking, assuring that most individuals will outlive any organization for which they work."[11]

Pink uses the transformation/demise of IBM as a prime example. IBM dominated the computer industry in its nascent years. It led the mainframe market with its vertically integrated solution of hardware, operating software, and application software. The saying back then was "nobody ever got fired for buying IBM."

All that changed when personal computers became pervasive in the 1980s. To catch up with the PC revolution, IBM outsourced the semiconductor chips to Intel and the operating system to Microsoft as it delivered its first personal computer in 1984. This was a crucial mistake—value in the computer industry was shifting from hardware to software.

IBM had always promised lifetime employment to their employees, but as their market position weakened, they could no longer uphold this promise. This is how Pink describes what happened next:

"The loyalty-for-security compact formed the foundation of corporate paternalism, and few companies worshipped it more reverently than IBM. For fifty years, across its far-flung operations,

IBM maintained a 'full-employment' policy. The company guaranteed its workers that it would never lay them off. Never. No matter how much business dropped, or the economy drooped, their jobs were safe. 'The policy was a religion,' one manager told *Fortune* magazine. 'Every personnel director who came in lived and died defending that practice. I tell you; this was like virginity.' But, by the early 1990s, IBM lifted its corporate window shades and saw a world starkly more challenging than it ever imagined. Upstart computer companies were gobbling market share. Globalization had opened new markets and let loose still more competitors. And a series of internal woes—strategic blunders and a slow-footed bureaucracy—made their external challenges even tougher. Faced with few alternatives, IBM abandoned its no-layoff policy, and in 1992 and 1993, whacked its payroll by 120,000 employees. The event was the workplace equivalent of the tumbling of the Berlin Wall just a few years earlier: everybody knew something monumental had just occurred, but nobody had a clue what would happen next."[12]

And it wasn't just at IBM where the promise of lifetime employment evaporated. The American economy was dominated by large corporations in the aftermath of World War II, but by the turn of the century in 2001, fewer than one in ten Americans worked in a Fortune 100 company.

For many American workers, this shift from a Fortune 100–dominated corporate economy to a much more diverse economy was tumultuous. But for those who were inclined to carve their own path, who never wanted a corporate life in the first place, it was an opportunity. It was easier to branch out on their own and create their own work environment, because for the first time there was a supporting infrastructure for doing so.

Scott Lawrence

"For me, it's all about freedom."

There is nothing in Scott Lawrence's early life to suggest he would become driven by the need for independence. He grew up the eldest of three siblings in a very religious Protestant family in Elkhart, Indiana. His family went to church three times a week: every Sunday morning, Sunday night, and Wednesday night.

Scott had an aunt and uncle who went to medical school at the University of South Carolina, and his family visited them through his childhood. Once he got out of high school, he decided at the last minute to go to college near them. As he puts it, "I looked at four schools in South Carolina and decided that I liked Charleston the best. They had the most beaches, golf courses, and girls."

After college, Scott got a job with Sears selling siding and windows across the East Coast for seven months before taking a job selling supply chain logistics for Airborne Express, which was eventually bought by DHL. Scott worked for Airborne Express in Charlotte and Chicago and then finally Dallas through different promotions.

By the time he got to Dallas he was making around $150,000 a year, still in his twenties and still single. He hated Dallas, though, and found a job in software sales to move back to Charleston. His territory was New York City, but he wanted to live in Charleston, so he just traveled to New York during the week.

Scott was exceptionally good at software sales—he only needed to work ten hours a week to make his quota. The rest of the time he was playing golf and hiking, or just hanging out with buddies. It was a good life, but he realized he had no passion for his work.

There was one clear sign of Scott's independent streak. The year before he made the switch to software sales, he took the year off work entirely and hiked the first 500 miles of the Appalachian Trial. When he was in college and when he was working his sales jobs, he loved going out to restaurants with his friends. While on the Appalachian Trail, he started to wonder if there was some way that he could make a career in the restaurant business.

Toward the end of 2008, right after the stock market crash, one of his friends in Charleston came over to his house and mentioned he was thinking of moving to Portland. Scott could keep his sales job going and live wherever he wanted. He thought, *Why not Portland?* Scott didn't know anyone in Portland, but he loved hiking and all of his hiking magazines were extolling the virtues of Oregon. Scott put his house up for sale and moved to Portland in February 2009. His friend never actually made the move because his employer wouldn't let him, but that didn't bother Scott much.

> **LESSON LEARNED:** Risk-takers will take a guaranteed hit just to get a chance at their goal.

After Scott moved to Portland, he took a trip that changed everything.

"I went on a kayaking trip with a couple of my best friends to Alaska," he explains, "a sea kayaking adventure north of Juneau. We fly into Juneau, we rent these sea kayaks with very little experience. I just like the water. I'm comfortable on it. We drive forty miles north of Juneau and the road just ends. All services, all electricity is gone, and it's just wilderness north for hundreds of miles. We put our kayaks in and paddle north for a handful of days and dodge some whales and have a couple of grizzly encounters. It was just an amazing experience.

"After five days in the wilderness, we go back to the brewery in Juneau and drink ourselves silly, get wild drunk. I was grinning ear to ear and my buddy, Bill, asked me, 'Why are you smiling so big?' I said, 'This is what I'm doing. I'm quitting my job and opening a brewery. I'm having so much fun. This is what I want my life to be.' My buddy's like, 'Sure you are.'

"I woke up the next day with a big headache, but with the knowledge that that's what I wanted to do. I called everybody I knew, posted it on Facebook that next day: 'Hey, I'm going to quit my job and open a brewery.' It just went from there."

LESSON LEARNED: Liberators make the jump when a feeling becomes an option.

Scott realized he was ready for his next gig, and that gig didn't involve working for anyone else. Two weeks after returning from Alaska, he did his version of market research to find a location for the brewery restaurant that he had decided to open.

"I was thinking that Portland people love having a brewery in their neighborhoods. I looked at the map and found where the two biggest gaps were, within the city limits, where there wasn't a brew pub. I rode my bike or drove to those two different areas. I remember it was Labor Day weekend. I found this awesome space in the northeast neighborhood of Portland that had a big circle around it. It didn't have a brew pub, and I found a building that still had dirt floors, but the exterior walls were awesome.

"I felt that I just needed to dive in and figure it out. So, I signed a five-year lease Labor Day weekend of 2009 on a 3,500-square-foot place that I was going to turn into a small brewery and restaurant."

> **LESSON LEARNED:** Risk-takers often burn the boats behind them to avoid retreating back to familiarity.

Scott was self-funding the brewery, and he hadn't saved enough money, so he kept his sales job until May 2010 when he opened the doors. Then he did what everyone with a corporate job dreams about. Scott was on a conference call with the entire sales team when his sales manager was harassing him about not filling out his expense report forms. He quit his job—on the spot, with everyone else on the phone. They tried to convince him to stay, but he told them, essentially, to take the job and shove it. In the middle of the Great Recession. It felt good.

Scott poured all his financial resources into the brewery. He sold his beloved Range Rover, rode his bike everywhere, emptied out his 401(k), and maxed out his credit cards. He was thirty-two years old, didn't have kids, and he could always go back to software sales. He wasn't worried.

In October 2010, shortly after the brewery opened, he met a girl in a parking garage in Portland. She was walking her brother's dog, which ran over and began licking Scott. They started chatting. She was a twenty-nine-year-old kindergarten teacher. Over the following ten days, they spent all their time together. At the end of those ten days, they both knew they were going to get married.

The business came close to going under many times in the first year. One day, about two months after he met his future wife, he tried to buy a $4.99 box of eggs from a grocery store using his debit card. It was declined.

A few nights later, they were at dinner, and his girlfriend could tell something was wrong. He told her he didn't know how he was going to make payroll the next Monday. She said, "Well, I believe in you, and I have $11,000 in my savings account. Would that help you?" She wrote a check that night to her new boyfriend of two months, emptying out her entire life savings.

Nine months after he opened the brewery it started to turn, slowly, in the right direction. The first nine months they had done almost exactly $60,000 per month in revenue. In the tenth month they did $63,000, then $66,000, then $70,000.

Scott decided they needed their own production facility to make beer. He didn't want to own just a small restaurant; his vision was that someday his friends on the East Coast would be able to buy his microbrew when they went to the grocery store. He met someone in Portland who pledged to loan him $1 million so that he could buy a facility. The guy gave him the first $325,000, but then reneged on the deal and demanded his money back.

Scott scrambled to source $1 million for the facility. His wife-to-be sold the only other asset she had, bonds that her grandmother had given her, to come up with $70,000. Scott started borrowing from other people, $20,000 at a time.

Soon after that, Scott entered the microbrew at a big tasting festival in Denver and won first place. It was his big break. The business took off from there. Today, Scott has over $20 million in annual revenue, two brewpubs, and one production facility. The business is highly profitable. There were plenty of obstacles along the way—frequently, he couldn't sleep because he was worried about making payroll. But Scott kept going.

Scott isn't that close to his father, who lacked confidence in him. "My mom says she always thought I could do it. I'm not real close with my dad, so I don't know what he thinks about me. Maybe he thinks I'm lucky."

He acknowledges the role of luck in success, but he also believes that boldness is often rewarded. "We hired one of the best-known brewers in town from another brewery. Other people said to him, 'Why are you leaving your secure position with a great company to join these guys who have no experience? You're crazy jumping to this new production facility based on the success of a small little brew pub.' But you know what? I think one of the things that was fortunate for us was that we didn't know enough. We didn't understand that we shouldn't take some of the risks that we did."

In our interviews, several risk-takers attributed their success to being young and not knowing what they didn't know. Brain researchers indicate people get more risk averse as they age. Many successful risk-takers see "not knowing" as an asset. They believe that, had they known all the risks, they may never have pursued the opportunity. Scott says that had he known at thirty-two what he knows now, at forty-one with a wife and two kids, he would never have taken the risks he did. He would have stayed in his comfortable sales gig. But he's glad he didn't know.

Scott believes that, since we only have one life, we should chase our dreams. He chased his dream when there was little evidence it could work, entering the brewery and restaurant industry with no experience. More than anything else, though, Scott's dream was about freedom.

"I just deleted Facebook from my phone two weeks ago. I don't care about social stuff at all. When I call my friends in the brewery business, they're like, 'We got approached by some of the big beer companies and wow, you could sell Breakside for $250 million." Something like that, I don't know. For me, it's all about freedom, including being free with my time. Right now, I'm rich by any standard I ever had; I get to do whatever I want, anytime I want. It's amazing. If I want to take the day and play with the kids, I can. With no more financial restrictions, I can go anywhere, do anything, at any time."

Jade Chang

"My philosophy is that every door is open until it's closed."

Jade Chang was born in Taiwan and moved to the United States when she was eighteen months old. She and her older brother and parents lived in the basement of a Catholic charity home for a few years, then they moved to a middle-class neighborhood in Connecticut. As immigrants, her parents were wired toward traditional, secure jobs—her father worked maintenance in a nuclear power plant for his whole career, and her mother in IT support.

As Jade puts it, "I was always a little rebellious." Her parents wanted her to play piano and violin, but she ended up learning jazz trumpet. She was also a tremendous athlete. A 400-meter runner, she received a full scholarship to the University of Texas. After she was injured in her freshman year of track, she took up rowing and weightlifting.

Jade realized she wasn't going to be a professional athlete. After college she took a job in tech consulting at PricewaterhouseCoopers, and then at Dell. She was bored, but she kept herself busy with triathlons and wakeboarding.

One day at Dell, Jade realized she didn't want to sit in a cubicle anymore. "My only desire was that I be self-employed," she explains. "If I had a child, I didn't want to ask someone else to take her to the doctor." It was that simple. Jade wanted her independence. She quit Dell and went to get an MBA in France. After one semester she realized she wasn't learning anything to help her start a business, so she quit the MBA program.

Jade returned to Austin. She convinced her brother to move into her place to help pay the rent. "It was super depressing. I remember waking up at nine in the morning thinking *I don't have anything to wake up for.* I needed to get my shit together. I thought *So, I have my leftover student loan. I cashed in my 401(k) from Dell, and I have a credit card. That's all I have to my name.*"

Jade was having a hard time explaining to her parents what she was doing with her life. "My parents thought I had lost it. I came back knowing that I wanted to start a business of some kind, but with no clue how to do that—none whatsoever."

Jade was good at recognizing her limitations. She knew many disruptive entrepreneurial businesses were started by creative types, but she was not a creative type. She just wanted to be self-employed in a business with real customers, where she could work hard and make enough cash to live.

So, of course, Jade decided to start an asphalt construction company. With zero experience in asphalt or construction. "If you don't have a construction or engineering background, you're limited on the kind of construction you can do. So, I chose the one thing anyone could learn, which was 'civil construction'—just asphalt and concrete."

Jade used her Dell severance, her 401(k), and credit cards to start a business she knew nothing about. She walked into an equipment dealer and asked, "What do I need to start paving roads?" She bought a dump truck for $20,000, a roller, a skid-steer, and a paving machine.

> **LESSON LEARNED:** When you don't
> know where to start, start somewhere.

Shortly afterwards, Jade met a guy in San Antonio—a guy who is now her husband and the father of her three children. San Antonio was growing fast, so she decided to move there to start her asphalt construction/road-paving business. She found her first employees—a foreman, a general manager, and the rest of the crew—on Craigslist.

Jade and her foreman started making cold calls to find who in San Antonio needed potholes filled. She's very action-oriented, but it did occur to her that she'd made a huge life shift that may or may not work out. "I went from being an athlete at UT and working worldwide as an IT consultant, traveling to Brazil, Malaysia and Ireland every month, to calling every apartment complex and shopping center in the yellow pages to see if they needed asphalt patching."

Jade's persistence started to pay off—or at least pay the bills. She took any project she could find, ranging from $1,000 to $10,000. In her first year, she generated $100,000 in revenue, positioning herself as a woman-owned business with the City of San Antonio and other general contractors. Then, she landed the AT&T Center—where the San Antonio Spurs play—as a large customer. By her fourth year in the asphalt construction business, she was doing $500,000 a year in revenue. Enough to pay her employees and her bills.

When the recession hit in 2009, Jade's business dropped to nothing. "I borrowed $90,000 from my mom," she recalls. "She had no money to loan me, so she took out a home equity line of credit. She didn't even tell my dad. So, I know that I have this loan to my mom, and that I also have these other loans . . . I am at this do-or-die moment, right? The recession is here. I either give up and go back to work, which I can do, but then I have to spend the rest of my life paying my mom back—or I have to figure something out pretty quick."

Jade had hit a Moment of Truth.

Because San Antonio is a military town, she tried to crack into military construction, encouraged by one of her fiancé's friends. She saw the money pouring in, but all the big players were getting the contracts. She couldn't get anyone's attention for big projects. So, she looked for opportunities too small for the big players, but meaningful to her.

Jade found her opportunity in a small Naval Air Station in Corpus Christi, Texas. "As luck would have it, they can't find a contractor to work there and do a good job. I bluff it and find a contracting officer called Charlotte, then annoy her to death until she agrees to meet with me and I beg her to give me a chance."

> **LESSON LEARNED:** Moments of Truth
> are opportunities to reinvent oneself.

"Charlotte gave me a $2,000 project to fix some floor tiles in an underground basement of an IT room. It cost me about $4,000 to do it by myself with a couple of other guys. I'm loading the baseboards from the basement into the trunk of my car and putting them into trash bins at my house. We lost money but did a good job.

"Then she gave me another project that's $13,000 to redo the masonry on the barbecue pits at the barracks. So, we did that, and made a grand on that. And then the next project is $27,000 to do retiling at the POW Museum."

Next Jade got the kind of break that you cannot plan for, but you can prepare to be in the right place at the right time. In 2010, a large hurricane from the Gulf of Mexico blew the roof off the Naval Air Station in Corpus Christi. Jade secured a $1.3 million contract to fix the roof.

Jade decided she liked the military construction market but needed to branch out beyond the small city of Corpus Christi. She visited the naval base in Ventura County, California, where she explained she was a small business contractor with an expertise in logistically difficult projects. She landed a $750,000 project to shore up underwater wood piles on a wharf that is a key naval transport to an island used for weapons testing. Given the regulations in California, many environmental issues factored into accomplishing the project.

Thus began a long and prosperous relationship with the naval base in Ventura County. Jade found her niche as a small business contractor for military construction. Contracts to inspect and repair fuel tanks for the Air Force, all over the world, followed. She landed Customs and Border Patrol as a customer in 2013.

As a small business contractor, Jade's business is regulated so that her revenue is capped at a $40 million five-year average. For the last three years, they've had to pick and choose their work to make sure they stay under that average. There are only seventy-six employees in the business. Like many constraints, this one has its upsides. Jade has been able to begin drawing cash flow out of the business, and she has hired a CEO who now manages the business for her day-to-day.

With her newfound cash and free time, Jade has begun investing in real estate and traveling more with her family. She's also returned to her passion for water sports, opening a boutique surf resort in Nicaragua and building another in Costa Rica. Her family's main residence is in Nicaragua, but they also have homes in LA and Hawaii.

> **LESSON LEARNED:** Risk-takers build entrepreneurial trees grown from the seedlings of hobbies.

In the last fifteen years, Jade has gone from being unemployed and sharing a rented house with her brother, to owning a successful military construction business, three homes, and focusing on her passion project of investing in surf resorts. Plus, she is married with three children. She's deeply appreciative of the support from her parents and her husband, but also fiercely independent. She and her husband keep all of their finances separate, except for their monthly contribution toward family expenses. That's the way she wants it. Her mom still can't believe she owns her own business.

Jade says, "I have this thing called the One Thing Rule. Which is that every day, I am just going to do one thing that gets me closer to my goal. It doesn't matter what that thing is. It could be as small as cold calling someone and leaving a message. My philosophy is that every door is open until it's closed."

Jeff Dudan

"Hurricane Andrew smashed it."

Jeff Dudan grew up in Schaumburg, Illinois, a suburb of Chicago. He was the middle child of three children. He says, quite simply, "It never occurred to me to get a job." He had one interview coming out of college, and he felt he knew a lot more than the interviewer. He knew right then that he would never work for anyone else.

Jeff believes many entrepreneurs feel they have nothing to lose because they lacked boundaries growing up. "They just do whatever they want to do," he says. "And a lot of times, when you get into business, that can be an asset."

Certainly, this perspective has been an asset for Jeff. He is careful about what he says about his childhood because he doesn't want to be overly negative about his parents. He made it clear several times during our discussion that he views his dad as a good guy, but he also acknowledges there was a lot of drinking in the house. By the time he was in high school, his parents had separated. He learned to run the house at an early age, out of necessity. Jeff hosted legendary Fourth of July parties with two hundred people at the house. He summarizes his childhood by saying, "It was not ideal, but it was what it was."

For Jeff, athletics were an escape from the dysfunctionality of his childhood. He was a poor student in high school, but he was an all-state football player. He broke the high school records as a receiver. Unfortunately, he wasn't fast enough to qualify for a NCAA Division I scholarship. He walked onto Northern Iowa's football team, but his grade point average was under 2.0, his dad's business wasn't going well, and he ran out of money for school. He went back home for two years and attended a junior college. He dedicated himself to football, became a tight end, did tons of weightlifting, and took a bunch of what he describes as "stupid" classes.

After junior college, Jeff was able to get several NCAA Division

II scholarship offers. When he visited Appalachian State in Boone, North Carolina, the coach told him to go home, pack his car, and come back in two weeks for the start of school. It wasn't too hard for him to pack everything that he owned in his car back then; he only had five T-shirts to his name.

Several things happened at Appalachian State that were formative to Jeff's future. First, his guidance counselor called him in and told him that his ACT scores were very high. Then his accounting teacher, Dr. Forsyth, started picking on him, presumably because he thought Jeff had potential. Jeff got the highest grade in the class on the first accounting test. For the first time in his life, it occurred to Jeff that he might be more than a jock, that he actually might be smart. No one had ever told him that before. He ended up graduating with honors and a degree in marketing.

On February 2 of his first year at Appalachian State, Jeff met his future wife, Traci, in a bar, which completely changed his life. They celebrate on February 2 every year, which has the advantage, Jeff points out, of buying cheaper flowers than on Valentine's Day.

Jeff was an entrepreneur from an early age. He washed cars and worked at a concrete company, in the Sears stockroom, and even in a dog costume at Chuck E. Cheese. He believes that early entrepreneurial experience is an indicator of future talent in starting businesses, a finding that is confirmed by several of our interviews.

In his first summer at Appalachian State, Jeff started a painting business. In the first year, they did $8,000 worth of business, and the next summer they did $56,000. By then, they were working for the property management company that managed all the student housing. They were painting thirteen to fourteen apartments per day and paying the painters $5 an hour in cash, plus all the pizza and soda they could drink. They had all the basketball players painting for them, which meant they could paint the ceilings without buying any ladders.

Jeff kept the painting business going after college for a while. He was good enough of a football player that he probably could have played in Europe, but he wasn't good enough to make it in the NFL. Plus, Traci still needed to finish school.

Then Jeff got his first big professional break. Here is how Jeff remembers it:

"Hurricane Andrew hits South Florida on August 24, 1992. We're winding down our painting season and a buddy calls me and says, 'Hey, this big hurricane just hit south Florida. Why don't you come down here? I'm working with a company; there's tons of work.' My partner and I got in our little four-cylinder Dodge pickup truck with the wooden pressure-treated ladder rack that we had built, and we drove down to Florida. When we got into Fort Lauderdale, and we crossed over this little rise, we drove the next two hours and there wasn't a roof on a house from there to the end of US Route 1. It was just massive devastation down there. It was crazy.

"We got some of our own jobs and the company that my buddy was working for said, 'Why don't you throw your jobs in with us? We've got a contractor's license. We'll split the profit and you can work for us.' After eighteen months, I ended up being the number-two guy to the person that ran the whole restoration operation. Several companies got together and had all their managers down there. I had a baptism of fire in insurance restoration. I was negotiating $7 million claims and talking in front of condominium boards; people were discussing their claims and how it was all going to work. I was dealing with lots of insurance companies."

Jeff learned the remediation, restoration, and reconstruction business, including insurance adjusting, from the ground up.

Literally. His marketing program was knocking on doors and meeting homeowners. When asked why he decided to move to South Florida, Jeff's answer was simple, "Well, Hurricane Andrew smashed it."

LESSON LEARNED: Every disaster is also an opportunity.

Jeff's partnerships generated $17 million of revenue in the Hurricane Andrew recovery. He became a pro at dealing with insurance companies. But his partnerships were also, in his words, "very, very ugly." Evidently, the disaster recovery business attracts lots of characters.

After Hurricane Andrew, he moved to Orlando for a year, but then he got engaged to Traci and moved back to Charlotte. Jeff was still a little rough around the edges and hadn't yet developed his Southern charm. Traci had to explain that he needed to buy her an engagement ring.

Fortunately, Charlotte was booming in the mid-nineties. Jeff created a business there that was focused on restoration from fire and wind damage, emergency services, and reconstruction. He called it Loss Control & Recovery:

"For about a month I stayed with my in-laws, but that didn't last. They were used to more structure than I was. I had no boundaries, so I ended up moving in with a buddy and crashing on his couch. I found an office that was out on Highway 16, outside of Charlotte where a guy was looking to rent just a conference room. I got to use a little thermal fax, and I got a couple of desks. I started getting some work in, and I did about $180,000 in sales the first year.

"I immediately went out and started knocking on doors, leveraging my knowledge from Florida in the insurance companies. I went to Nationwide Insurance; they have a big claims office. There's this young claims manager who's about my age and he's huge. I sit down with him and find out he played for Clemson. I played for App State. We played them and they beat the crap out of us, but we were on the field at the same time. He says, 'Okay, come with me. I'm going out on a claim.' We go on a roof claim, he does the estimate, then says to the customer, 'This is who I recommend doing the job.' I'm like, 'Okay, we'll do it.' The customer says, 'Okay, that's fine with me.' She writes the check, he hands it to me and says, 'Don't screw it up.'

"I go to the shingle supply place. I find this deadbeat roofer guy who will do it at a price that'll allow me to make some money. The first day on the job, he drives this little dump truck down the property line and breaks off every branch of the neighbor's Bradford pear tree. For a $2,200 job, I ended up having to pay a tree surgeon to deal with these neighbors. They kept calling me every day. I ended up losing probably $2,000 on that job. I went home to my wife and said, 'Don't worry. We're going to make it up on volume.'

"Then we built a team. The first full year in business, I did $992,000 in sales in Charlotte."

Jeff is modest as he describes what happens next. He says that if he wrote a book, it would be called *Too Stupid to Fail*. But he always had a vision for the business. He remembers sitting down with his first hire in Charlotte, Ray, a good guy who had fallen on hard times. He explained to Ray how they could evolve the business into a franchise model. Jeff believed that if they could create a brand and a franchise model, they could generate profits from someone else running the operation, as long as they had the right franchise owners. That appealed to him.

Jeff rebranded his business, calling it AdvantaClean. He built a sales organization. He stopped focusing on fire restoration, shifting his attention to the more profitable environmental services: mold remediation, emergency wastewater, mold sampling and testing, and air quality.

He continued to chase disasters, doing over $40 million of business from Hurricane Katrina. By 2006 he was doing about $11 million a year of very profitable revenue in environmental services.

Then he did the unthinkable. He always wanted to turn the environmental services business into a franchise model where franchise owners ran their own jobs. But doing so would cannibalize his business where they were directly responsible for the jobs. To become a major franchise operator, he had to kill his existing revenue stream.

Jeff plunged in anyway. He started experimenting with the franchising model in 2006 by selling off three of his existing locations to franchisees, shifting fully to franchising in 2009. The cash was tight, because he needed to fund his franchising start-up, but it worked . . . eventually. Franchising businesses don't pay off until they reach scale and, according to Jeff, only 5 percent of franchising businesses ever reach one hundred franchises, but if they reach scale, they are highly profitable. Jeff decided to take that bet.

We asked Jeff if he knew going into it how risky creating a franchise operation would be. His answer didn't surprise us:

"Of course not. We didn't have anybody that had any franchising experience in the building for the first five years. We just figured it all out ourselves. Like I said, *too stupid to fail.* But here's the other thing: it was also brilliant because we did a call center that nobody would've recommended—nobody does it like us. It ended up being our competitive advantage that enabled me to sell the business for more money because our franchise owners don't have overhead in their office answering the phones.

"We're one of the few franchisors in the country that actually know every job, because most of these companies do it the old way. If you don't start it that way, franchisees will develop their own software, have their in-laws working in the office, answering their own phones. Our franchises have never answered their own phones. We crush it in sales. Last year, we drove 220,000 inbound calls and booked 25,000 appointments on jobs for our franchise owners. That was so hard, but it was a competitive advantage for our brand."

Once Jeff got a handle on the franchising model, he began to scale the business. He started doing between eighteen and twenty-four franchises a year. By 2018, he was up to one-hundred thirty ownership groups in thirty-seven states, less than ten years after committing to the franchising model. By then, big investors were trying to buy fast-growing services franchising businesses with great marketing and call center operations—like Jeff's.

On January 1, 2019, Jeff sold his entire business for a lot of money. For the first time in his life, he had the opportunity to take some time to think through his next step—and the financial resources to do what he wants.

Jeff took a huge risk, killing his successful services business to create a franchising model. But Jeff saw what others didn't: to deliver service with high customer satisfaction, he needed local ownership. Jeff couldn't deal with every neighbor's complaint. Franchising was the only way to get that level of ownership.

Jeff believes that people's values aren't measured in what they say, but rather what they do. Or, as he puts it, "what they are willing to tolerate." Right about the time when Jeff was chasing Katrina, he and Traci had their third child. Jeff realized he wasn't willing to tolerate being an absentee father; he was going to be there for his kid's school plays and athletic events. To pull that off, he had to create the franchising model.

Jeff emphasizes that his own parents were good people, but he wasn't okay with his own kids growing up like he did—with no rules and not that much parental engagement. Jeff decided that he was going to be home when it counted.

> **LESSON LEARNED:** Values aren't what you say, they are about what you are willing to tolerate.

Himanshu Sareen

*"I had this desire to do my own thing. I didn't
know what it was going to be, but I knew
that I wanted to run my own thing."*

Himanshu Sareen has sought freedom his entire life. He grew up in New Delhi, India, but now lives in New York City. Both of his parents are retired teachers. Himanshu was always interested in business and wanted to be an entrepreneur, even though there were no role models in his family. Teachers are well respected but often are not well compensated, and this was especially true in India.

Himanshu grew up in a happy family, but when he was ten his fourteen-year-old brother contracted leukemia and succumbed to the disease. His family didn't have the language or emotional communication skills to deal with the tragedy at that time. They plowed ahead with their daily lives. Himanshu saw other wealthier people in India get cancer and survive. As a grieving teenager, he wondered if they could have saved his brother's life if his family had more money. Himanshu knows this was likely not true, but the tragic experience shaped how he thought about money and wealth.

In New Delhi, Himanshu went to a Catholic school run by Irish brothers, the same school his father attended. Half his classmates were subsidized by the church and came from very modest backgrounds, with their tuition covered by the Irish brotherhood, and the other half were wealthy. Himanshu was somewhere in the middle and felt out of place. He had a passion for business and wanted to be an entrepreneur.

Entrepreneurship seemed to be in Himanshu's blood. When he was twelve, he started a business renting out comic books. He borrowed them from the local library and rented them out. The business was simple, and Himanshu made more money than any twelve-year-old would know what to do with.

Himanshu was interested in technology and taught himself. He eventually earned a business degree in college in India—at the time technology and the web were at such nascent stages that he did not think he could learn a lot from his teachers as they themselves were learning, but knew he needed to learn financial accounting to run a business.

After college, Himanshu took a job with a large US-based agriculture conglomerate. His recollection is succinct: "I worked with them for a short while—I didn't enjoy what I was doing at all, so I quit and decided to start a company."

LESSON LEARNED: Liberators don't tolerate boredom for long.

Himanshu got a job with a foundation supporting the corporate social responsibility (CSR) movement. He observed that big companies were bidding to build software to support the CSR reporting of the foundation, and they were charging a lot of money. Himanshu knew he could build the software on his own for far less. He went to his boss and offered to take on the IT project for half of the lowest bid. His boss took him up on the offer, and Himanshu had his first IT services client.

Himanshu moved into his parents' basement to bootstrap his company. His first clients came from his ex-boss. He caught the full brunt of the dot-com crash in late 2000, and many of his startup clients did not pay their bills. Then, in 2006 when Himanshu was twenty-eight, the building that served as their data center had a major fire, and one-third of the building was destroyed.

Himanshu just kept working and building his client base. He started the business to fund a graduate education in the United States, but Himanshu realized he just wanted to keep building the business. Instead of moving to the States, he got an MBA in India through a weekend program.

A few years after he re-built the data center from the fire, Himanshu saw big challenges emerging with his business. Large competitors like Infosys and Wipro were expanding their market share. And with no barriers to entry, more and more IT services companies were popping up, and his basic IT services offering was being commoditized. He built software to the customer's specification, but Himanshu's company didn't have any input into the specs, and they didn't own any of the intellectual property. Himanshu knew he had to differentiate or suffer being a low-cost, low-value business.

Himanshu's adventure-seeking nature kicked in, and he decided the only way to build the kind of business he wanted was to move to New York. This seemed to some like a crazy idea. He was doing extremely well by New Delhi standards; he had a big house and a chauffeur. By now he had a wife and a young daughter. He knew no one in New York. He had no immigration status or papers in place. He had built the business in India from scratch, and he was putting everything at risk.

Many would-be risk-takers are burdened by what we call the Right Time Fallacy. Himanshu felt no such burden, which freed him to take risks that others would advise against.

KEY CONCEPT—RIGHT TIME FALLACY: The notion, unsupported by our research, that the risk-taker should wait for "the right time" in their life to take a risk.

Himanshu decided to move. At his company's annual all-employee meeting in early 2010, he got up and told everyone he was moving. He explained he had confidence in his team to keep the Indian branch going, and he thought the move to New York was the only way the business could fulfill its potential.

By the end of 2010, he was in New York on an L visa (an intracompany transfer). He rented a corporate apartment and had no idea what to do next. His wife and daughter stayed back in India that first year, and Himanshu spent considerable time on flights between New York and New Delhi.

Himanshu knew he was starting over. He didn't mind that; in fact, it energized him. The only way Himanshu knew how to start a business was by bootstrapping it, and he had confidence that he could do that in New York. He gave himself $50,000 and a year to get the New York business off the ground. Plus, he genuinely believed that the business in India would not exist in five years unless he redefined it.

> **LESSON LEARNED:** Risk-takers are
> brutally honest with themselves.

Himanshu used temporary office space in New York and went to meetups to make contacts, 95 percent of which were a waste of time. He experimented with digital marketing, building an online presence, and learning how digital advertising works. He sensed it would be an important market opportunity. The meetups led to more meetups, and eventually Himanshu found his first real client, a major events company.

This events company was the perfect early client. They were

well behind the technology curve and knew it. They had physical capacity constraints as well as legacy IT infrastructure that limited their growth potential. They understood that a stronger digital presence was a possible way—perhaps the only way—to grow their business. They had already experienced catastrophic technology failures and wanted to stop blowing their money on tech.

If this events company was the perfect client, Himanshu was the perfect person for them. They needed someone they could trust, someone who would listen to them and understand their needs, and Himanshu was desperate for his first digital transformation customer.

He started out with a small project: a tech audit to assess how they made decisions and where they had gone wrong so far. He wanted to build trust in a mutual learning effort, but also create a broader game plan for moving forward. He hired analysts in New York and established a home office. Himanshu lost money on the initial project, but it laid the foundation for the future direction of the business.

Himanshu presented his findings to the entire executive team. He explained why he thought they were failing and laid out a digital roadmap for the next five years.

The management team bought into the vision. They hired Himanshu and his new team, and Himanshu used teams in both New York and India to deliver his company's first end-to-end digital transformation project. Three years into their relationship, the events company had tripled its top line revenue, and Himanshu was well on the path of reinventing his own business.

Himanshu saw the power of digital transformation and reconfigured his business to cater to this growing demand. He realized the big paying customers would be in the United States, and many of those customers would be in New York. He built a team in New York skilled in digital strategy, analysis, and customer experience—a new age digital solutions company. He realized that India would be better suited to support that work, so he let all of his Indian customers go and turned his operations there into a back-office.

From 2010 to 2013, Himanshu completely transformed his own business by helping his clients with their own digital transformation initiatives. What stands out is how brutally honest he was about his own business. He clearly saw the problems with being an outsourcing company based in India. When his team was far away from the customers in the United States, interacting only through Skype or FaceTime, they would just build whatever the customer wanted. If it was the right thing to build, they would build it. If it was the wrong thing to build, they would also build it. Himanshu realized his team needed to be in the same room as the customer to have direct, honest conversations. That was the only way to achieve better results.

There was another advantage to having a presence in New York. By having talented people working directly with the customer, they could change their pricing model to that of value-based pricing. Himanshu saw that if he could figure out how to do 80 percent of revenue in the United States and 80 percent of the work in India, he could be much more scalable. In the year before our interview, he'd grown revenue 20 percent without adding any headcount. This unique structure is hard for competitors to replicate.

Himanshu faced personal obstacles in his move to New York. Himanshu was building the business, traveling back and forth between New York and India.

There was also the issue of his immigration status. Himanshu came to the United States on an intracompany transfer, but he didn't fully understand the immigration laws. Right as he was in the middle of building his US business, he had to move back to India. He was spending a lot of money on immigration lawyers and not getting any results. It was a difficult time for him and his family. Eventually, Himanshu grew frustrated with his lawyers, spent a month researching immigration laws, wrote his own application, had his status reinstated, and moved back to New York.

During our research, we found that many risk-takers have a fascinating view of obstacles. Above all, when they get stuck, instead of doubling down, they consciously choose to *do something different*.

Like all risk-takers, Liberators have fears, but they don't let those fears dominate their lives. They make big decisions with their heads and their hearts (Livewith Two). And they take ownership of their lives, sometimes in dramatic fashion.

Himanshu uprooted his entire life when he moved from India to New York City. Scott Lawrence took longer to quit his software sales job and start a microbrewery, but the seeds of his independence were planted in rural Indiana. Jade Chang hit rock bottom several times, but her simple decision to start an asphalt construction company, about which she knew nothing, "because I wanted to be self-employed," changed her life. And Jeff Dudan, who started out chasing hurricanes to find business, eventually created a national franchise because he wanted to be at home to provide his kids the kind of life that he didn't have.

At their core, Liberators are driven by the need to create their own life without giving up huge chunks of their existence to a corporation.

We met several other Liberators in our research. They were all unwilling to live by the rules of the mainstream corporate world and were determined to write their own life stories. Even if their decisions did not always lead to perfect results, they focused their energies on creating the kind of world they wanted to live in.

These are the free agents that Daniel Pink foresaw in 2001.

CHAPTER SEVEN

Survivors

Risk-takers tend to have significant life survival skills. They persevere when things get tough, even relishing tough times as opportunities to prove their mettle and learn more about themselves. They don't allow obstacles to paralyze them. They understand all of us experience failure and heartbreak; what matters is how we pick ourselves back up off the ground.

Then there are the risk-takers who find a way to create a meaningful life no matter what life throws at them. We call them Survivors.

We met several Survivors who lost parents at an early age.

For example, Steve Muntean grew up in Chicago, and his parents were separated when he was young. He lived with his mom, who was a single working mother with chronic kidney disease and working as a medical malpractice reporter. Steve was used to doing things on his own as a kid. At ten, he figured out how to get around downtown Chicago and to find something to eat. He spent many nights by himself because his mom was working, or sometimes because she was in the hospital.

His mom did everything for Steve to make sure he learned how to survive in the world, from enrolling him in etiquette classes to a comedy training program at The Second City. She was in and out of the hospital often with her kidney disease, especially with pneumonia. None of the drugs seemed to be working. One night when he was thirteen, she died in her sleep.

Losing his mom so suddenly and at such an early age made Steve feel powerless. The rest of his extraordinary life choices have been about reclaiming his power and using that power to help others.

Steve finished high school in the Chicago suburbs with his dad's new family. Immediately after graduating, he moved to Florida where he started a tech company and sold it by the age of twenty-five.

Now he had the means to help others, but he needed a way to do so. He decided to get trained to become a cop. During his training, he realized that the security industry itself was broken, and he decided to apply his entrepreneurial skills. Now, still in his thirties, he's combined his passion to help others with those skills and created several successful private security firms in Florida.

Like Steve Muntean, Margaret Mueller has transcended tragedy in her childhood.

"I'm a first-generation college graduate," she tells us. "My dad was a mechanic. My mom stayed at home. I was the youngest of four and there are ten years between me and my sister. So, I was the late life 'oops' baby, which has a lot of implications as I go through life.

"When I was three, my first brother went away to college. When I was five, my next brother left. When I was nine, my sister married and moved out. And then my mom died tragically in an auto accident when I was eleven. So, then it was just my father and me in the house."

Margaret's father wasn't particularly supportive of her education, but she knew she needed to get out of their hometown. She worked hard to fund her own education and ended up getting a PhD in psychology.

Margaret had zero role models of successful career women during her childhood, so she focused her academic career solely on that topic: the study of women who create successful paths. Today, she is CEO of a large networking nonprofit called the Executive Club of Chicago.

The Supreme Court Justice Ruth Bader Ginsburg may be best known today as a liberal court justice, but she was also a fiercely independent Survivor. Above all else, she found a way to keep doing the work that she loved as long as she could—in the face of tragedies and obstacles that could have easily derailed a lesser person.

Ruth's mother died of cancer the day before she graduated from high school, but not before she left an indelible imprint on her daughter. Her mother, Celia Amster Bader, gave Ruth two pieces of advice before she died—the first was to always be a lady, and the second was much less conventional advice for women in the 1950s—to always be independent. Even in the eyes of her toughest critics, there can be little doubt that Ruth followed both. Throughout the rest of her life, Ruth often said that her mother was the most intelligent person she ever met.

RBG married her husband, Martin, who later became a prominent tax attorney, shortly before she entered Harvard Law School in 1956. She was one of only nine women in a class of five-hundred men. The law school dean invited all nine women to his home for dinner and asked them, "Why are you at Harvard Law School, taking the place of a man?" Ruth hesitated and stated that she simply wanted to be able to talk to her husband Marty about his work. It was perhaps the last time in her storied career RBG was at a loss for words.

Marty was diagnosed with testicular cancer soon thereafter, and Ruth began attending his classes also (he was a year ahead of her at Harvard Law) to take notes for him. When Marty graduated and took a job in New York City, Ruth asked the dean at Harvard if she could attend her last year at Columbia and still get a Harvard degree. He denied her request.

Ruth graduated tied for first in her class at Columbia Law School in 1959, but she had difficulty finding employment. As she said in her 1993 speech accepting the Supreme Court nomination at the White House, there was "not a law firm in the entire city of New York that bid for my employment as a lawyer when I earned my degree."

After law school, a Harvard law professor recommended Ruth for a Supreme Court clerkship to the famed Justice Felix Frankfurter. Frankfurter rarely turned down such a recommendation, but he rejected Ruth. He reportedly protested "she has a couple of kids, and her husband has been ill, and you know that I work you guys very, very, hard, and I do curse sometimes." Ruth had only one child at the time, and Frankfurter was known to never curse.[13]

A true Survivor, RBG was undeterred by these setbacks. She went onto an academic career at Rutgers and Columbia and argued several cases before the Supreme Court as a volunteer attorney for the ACLU advocating for gender equality. In August 1993 she was appointed a Supreme Court Justice by Bill Clinton.

In 1999, RBG was diagnosed with colon cancer. Despite undergoing chemotherapy and radiation treatment, she did not miss a day on the bench over the next ten years. She began working out with a personal trainer, and at age eighty she was able to do twenty push-ups.

Colon cancer, however, was only the first of RBG's five bouts with cancer. In 2009, she underwent surgery for pancreatic cancer; in 2014 she had a stent placed in one of her arteries; in 2018 she fractured three ribs while working out; in January 2019 she finally missed her first day of work as a Supreme Court Justice when she had an operation for cancer in her lung.

Ruth and Marty had a famously close and supportive marriage, and some court observers expected her to step down after Marty died a week after their fifty-sixth wedding anniversary in 2010.

Ruth did not step down. Instead, she simply kept working. She was known to leave voicemails for her clerks in the middle of the night. As the Court itself turned more conservative, she became known for her well-crafted dissents.

She once said of her work, "I just try to do the good job that I have to the best of my ability, and I really don't think about whether I'm inspirational. I just do the best I can."

Survivors helped us realize that risk-takers don't wait for the perfect time to take a risk. There is no such perfect time.

Robin Greene

"I could take what little money I had left and be a force
for positive change. So that's what I decided to do."

Robin Greene was a military brat. She lived all over the United States growing up and even spent time on a merchant marine ship sailing around South America. After high school in San Antonio and college at Baylor University, she moved to Dallas where she met her husband. She has lived in the Dallas area for more than twenty-five years.

Robin began working in healthcare technology companies, and eventually in smaller start-up companies. She learned she has strong leadership and operations skills. She ended up running a healthcare analytics company that helped insurance companies analyze hospital reimbursement rates and patients' buying patterns.

The company grew and was acquired by a larger Goldman Sachs–backed healthcare company right before the stock market crash in 2008. Robin signed a three-year contract to continue to run the acquired company for the new parent company and acquired several other companies during that time. She was busy, successful, and made life-changing money from the sale of her company. Robin was on a fast career track in the growing health-care data analytics industry.

By 2013 Robin was ready for a change. She was burned out after many years of building and running companies. She was married with two kids. It wasn't that she was done with her career, but she was definitely ready for some time off. She resigned from her position and started thinking about what to do with her new-found downtime.

In mid-September, two weeks before she was to leave her job, Robin and her husband spent a Friday night in a luxury boutique hotel in downtown Dallas and left the two kids with their nanny. It was her husband's birthday and shortly after their sixteenth wedding anniversary. When they returned home on Saturday, she went online. One of her goals during her year off was do more household tasks, including paying the bills.

Robin logged into their bank and was dumbfounded. There was no money in any of their bank accounts. She had made a ton of money from the sale of her company, and it hadn't been that long since she had checked the accounts. Her first instinct was that the accounts had been hacked. She turned to her husband and said, "Oh my God. There's no money in any of these bank accounts." She expected him to be shocked. He was not shocked.

Robin turned back to the computer screen, processing her husband's lack of response. She could hardly believe what she was seeing. She turned back to him, uttered some profanities, and said, "You need to tell me where the money is." He told her that he had been gambling. She didn't know what to think. It didn't make sense—whenever they went to Vegas, they spent $200 on slots and when it was gone, they were done. It was totally out of character for her husband to lose their entire net worth on gambling.

Robin spent the next two weeks, the last two weeks of her high-paying job, in a fog. She was trying to be the supportive spouse, helping her husband with a gambling addiction problem, while processing that all their money was gone—and she was about to be out of a job. Then she found a vape pen in her kid's playroom. At first, she didn't even know what it was, but she didn't think her kids—then ten and twelve—were smoking anything.

When her husband came home that night, she said to him as he walked in the door, "I believe there is more to your story." He quickly admitted he'd been unfaithful. That was the moment when she realized the issue was much, much bigger than a vape pen. She asked if he was being unfaithful with someone she knew, and he said no. He said he was being unfaithful with prostitutes. As Robin says in retelling what happened next, "You can imagine there were a whirlwind of emotions going on." She kicked her husband out of the house that night.

Her husband became suicidal. His family found him and committed him to a facility to stabilize the situation. Robin wasn't sure what to tell her kids. She didn't want to dump the toxicity of the situation on her children. She finally said, "Daddy has to be in a hospital right now because he's going through some challenges and being there will help him get better."

In the middle of all this, Robin had to put down the family dog, which had been a wedding gift to her husband. She didn't miss the symbolism—she was simultaneously euthanizing the family dog and her marriage.

Robin was dazed and confused, dealing with a financial and marital betrayal beyond her imagination. She visited her husband in the treatment facility and found him practically catatonic. She could tell that he knew she was there, but he couldn't engage with her or anyone else. She knew her marriage was over.

On her way home that day, Robin's nanny called to tell her the house was flooding. When Robin got home, water was streaming out the front door. She didn't even know how to shut the water off; that was the kind of thing her husband always did. She told the nanny, "You need to get the kids and take them away; I'm about to combust."

After the nanny and the kids left, Robin had a heated discussion with God. She told God that she couldn't take anymore and collapsed to her knees in the pool of water. She felt a gentle force on the back of her neck, pulling her up to her feet, and simply stating, "You are going to be alright; I am trying to show you something." She answered God out loud with a few choice obscenities. "Alright, you've got my attention." It was then that a neighbor showed up from way down the street, with a bottle of wine and two glasses. The neighbor said, "I can hear you screaming from down the street. I think you need a friend. What's going on?" Robin told her the whole story.

Meanwhile, the treatment facility ran Robin's husband through all sorts of tests—physical, psychological, even an MRI. All manner of clinical professionals got involved. Robin was hoping they would find an operable brain tumor, meaning her husband could be saved and there would be a clear reason for all of his stupid decisions.

At long last, the clinicians at the facility told Robin their diagnosis. "Your husband is a sex addict."

"No," she protested. "That's what Tiger Woods is, not my husband." They gave her a crash course on addiction and recommended that he be transferred to another facility.

Robin was, of course, still in shock and trying to salvage some aspect of her life. She was also trying to protect her kids. She and her kids visited the new facility. When they got there, the clinical professionals shared vivid, inappropriate details with her children. Robin maintained a poker face until she no longer could, and then she abruptly left to go home.

Robin thought about suing the facility for their behavior with her children. As she remembers it, "I got to a place where I was at a crossroads where I could take a punitive measure with that facility and sue them for some of the things that had happened and the damage that had been done—stuff I was now trying to undo with outside clinicians, especially with my kids. Or I could take what little money I had left and be a force for positive change. So that's what I decided to do."

It could have gone either way. Robin was facing the loss of her marriage, destruction of her net worth, a flooded house, and clinical professionals sharing intimate details of her husband's sex addiction with her young children. Most people in her situation would have folded their cards up, gone home, and hid under the covers. Robin didn't do that. Instead, she took a truly awful situation and looked for any possible silver lining to turn it around.

This is what conscious life survivors do. They realize that life throws us all curveballs and that life isn't fair. Robin found a way to take personal responsibility for the rest of her life, even as others around her were being terribly irresponsible.

As Robin considered what to do next, she recalled what her investors told her, "Whatever you want to do next, call us first." It was time to make that phone call. To get through her own trauma, Robin had met some incredible clinical professionals who wanted to make a difference in the lives of those with addictions. But the management systems and culture of facilities didn't support clinical staff doing their best work. Robin realized she could help prevent other families from suffering as hers had.

Over the next three years, armed with funding from her original investors, Robin co-created an innovative residential facility treating substance and process addictions. It's an intense, family-oriented program to help the addict and their family understand exactly what addiction is. It took about a year to construct the facility.

Close to 1,000 people and their families have now been treated. It's an addiction rehab clinic and also much more. Robin has learned that addictions aren't just caused by physical pain and trauma, they are also caused by emotional pain that is harder to see and understand. Often the source of the emotional pain goes back to childhood, as it did in the case of Robin's ex-husband.

Robin had the courage to look at her own role in what led to the demise of her marriage. She realized that her addiction was work. While she was physically available to her husband, she often wasn't emotionally available. Nor was he emotionally available to her. Looking back, she saw they were living lives disconnected from each other and that at least some of that was her responsibility. Finally, she understood that to move on with her life, she had to forgive. It takes a big person to deal with everything that Robin was and forgive the person whose behavior caused so much turmoil. Robin is that big person.

In founding this innovative treatment facility, Robin didn't just create a healing facility. She also created a teaching facility, one that freely shares its practices and knowledge with other treatment centers. The facility offers continuing education units (CEUs) to clinicians from competing facilities so they can learn what they are doing. Robin wouldn't have it any other way. She speaks across the country and across the world on what addiction is and how to deal with a loved one who is struggling with addiction. It's not just a business—it's her life calling.

> **LESSON LEARNED:** Risk-takers can turn painful experiences into positive initiatives for others.

"Our knee-jerk reaction when someone keeps falling off the wagon is to ostracize them. And that's really one of the worst things you can do. You need to have healthy boundaries. But we teach people how to have those healthy boundaries and still be supportive and understand that it's not as simple as, 'Don't go buy that bottle of vodka and you won't drink.' At some point, it becomes a deep physiological and psychological need to sustain life, much like oxygen is a basic need for human survival. And it's the only way they know to escape whatever is haunting them, whatever's hurting them, whatever pain they have.

"We all, as human beings, have trauma in our life. Trauma is not just sexual or physical abuse. Trauma can be the divorce of your parents, a financial crisis, a natural disaster, being bullied in school. Trauma is everywhere. We all experience it. We collectively use that word. But what might be traumatic for you might be nothing for me and vice versa. So, it's difficult for someone to sit in judgment of someone saying, 'Why do you drink? Because your parents got divorced?' Like, 50 percent of our generation have divorced parents. Well, that's a punitive way to address someone. Understanding that their family divorce impacted them significantly— enough that they're choosing unhealthy ways to escape—is key.

"The other piece is we treat complex co-occurring diagnoses. Along with addiction, you often find depression, anxiety, PTSD, bipolar, schizophrenia, and dissociative identity disorder to name a few. We work with the complex cases. We have everybody from the occasional binge drinker on up to the main line heroin or meth user at our facility. We don't separate by drug of choice because it doesn't matter that you do cocaine or that person does wine or that person does heroin. It doesn't matter. You just have a different drug of choice, but you're still using it for the same reason—to medicate some sort of pain.

"We have a robust curriculum that we put in place where these folks are seeing individual therapists three times a week, much more than most facilities. We have all masters-degree-level clinicians. We have a medical director, a psychiatric nurse practitioner. We work on looking at individuals' previous diagnoses to see if they've been misdiagnosed. We also look at their medications and try to figure out how to get them off the stuff they don't need. We feed them nutrient-dense, high-quality food so we can repair their bodies from the damage of drugs and alcohol. We teach them balance. I teach the leadership development group where we talk about life purpose, skills, and things that could be stressful for them or prevent them from living their best life."

Robin has turned her own life trauma into an innovative, mission-driven, for-profit care facility that is focused on transforming lives. In the process, she has learned how to forgive in the most difficult circumstances imaginable. She has found her life calling from the ashes of her own catastrophic life turmoil.

Tana Greene

"You have to make a choice whether you want to be a victim or a survivor."

Tana Greene (no relation to Robin) grew up in a *Leave It to Beaver*–type of family that sat down to dinner together every night at six o'clock. They lived in Chesapeake, Virginia, where her father was a United States Coast Guard officer and her mother a stay-at-home mom. Tana was an honor roll student.

When she was in the ninth grade and dating the most popular boy in her high school, Tana got pregnant. Having grown up in a

Southern Christian family, she will never forget what it was like to tell her mother the news.

"My first words to her were, 'You're not going to love me anymore,'" Tana says. "She turned to me and said, 'Oh yeah, I think I will.' I said, 'No, I don't think so.' She says, 'Just tell me what it is. I think I already know.' I said, 'I think I'm pregnant.' She says, 'I'm pretty sure you are too.' I said, 'How do you know that?' And she replies, 'Well, you've gotten sick every morning for the last two weeks.' She wrapped her arms around me and says, 'I was so afraid I was going to be too old to be a grandmother.' Now, you know that's not what she was thinking. But in that moment, she gave me that unconditional love to make a decision."

Tana decided to get married, and two weeks later she walked down the aisle. She hoped she would live happily ever after, but it was not to be. Soon after she quit high school and had her son, she realized she was in a domestic violence situation.

Her husband had a horrible temper. "If I said something he thought was stupid, he would push me out the back door in the winter, lock the door behind me, and leave me out there for two hours. Or he'd lock me in a closet when people came over to the house. It was insane. The physical things that he did are just unimaginable for anybody to go through."

Less than two years into the marriage, her husband beat up Tana, and she showed up at her parents' house in bad shape. Her mom took Tana to a counselor at the local YWCA. After a week of daily therapy, the counselor told Tana, "There's nothing wrong with you. You really just have to make a choice whether you want to be a victim or a survivor."

Tana made the decision to be a survivor. She left her marriage with a child and without a high school degree or a job. Tana wrote down her goals:

"Finish high school (and not with a GED)."

"Get some form of higher education."

"Own my own home before age twenty-five."

"Have my own business before age thirty."

"Meet my knight in shining armor."

This was Tana's first, and most important, Moment of Truth.

Tana and her son moved back with her parents. She finished high school in three years and enrolled in a trade school—Commonwealth College in Virginia Beach—to learn shorthand, typing, and accounting. The day she graduated from that school, she found a job as an executive secretary at Econo Lodge, a hotel chain. She was eventually hired as a media buyer by Econo Lodge's ad agency.

A year into working for the ad agency, Tana got a call from the admissions director at Commonwealth College, asking her if she would be willing to recruit new students. At the time, Tana was getting $15 per week in child support and making $8,000 a year. The recruiting job was commission only, but Tana took it. In her first six months, she made $30,000. In the next four years, Tana grew the school's enrollment from 60 to 600 students.

> **LESSON LEARED:** Taking a risk on yourself is often the best kind of risk to take.

Tana bought her first house at age twenty-two for $56,000.

The next year, when Tana was twenty-three and her son was seven, she went on a blind date and met her knight in shining armor. Her new boyfriend was an engineer in the nuclear power industry. He eventually asked her to marry him and move to Southern California where he had a consulting project. Tana didn't hesitate. "It was a no-brainer. He was just the kindest person—totally the opposite of my first husband—somewhere between introverted and extroverted and just always kind. It felt right from the very beginning. He was a nuclear consultant, so he was all over the place: New Jersey, Georgia, Florida. We never lived in the same town, so we would see each other when he was between gigs, basically. He asked me to marry him. And then off we went to California. It's all about taking risks."

They lived in Southern California for three years, during which Tana worked as director of admissions for a for-profit trade school. When she was twenty-six, she had sixteen sales reps working for her. After several years, the school got a new VP of admissions. He told Tana that he thought women were too emotional and should not be working.

Tana was a different person in her late twenties—she wasn't going to put up with a man dictating her place in the world. Tana quit her job the following week.

"I decided that I wanted to be a headhunter. I don't know where that came from. I just thought I would be really good. I loved helping people get jobs. I loved helping people get trained because I got such a thrill out of it when they got their job. We had a 98 percent placement rate coming out of these schools. These were people that were never going to get out of a factory, but they had some kind of skill. And we placed them in jobs—it just felt good. It felt like a purpose. I thought, *If I become a headhunter, I can directly impact people going to work.*

"I called the top three headhunting companies in Southern California. I called the proprietor and I said, 'Can I come and interview you? I just want to understand this industry.' I ended up with job offers because of my past success. My boss wanted to start a temporary division for paralegals and secretaries to complement the insurance executives and attorneys he was placing. He offered me a job to come in to set up that business.

"About ninety days into doing the research, I came home, and I said to my husband, 'This is what I want to do for the rest of my life. I want to own a staffing company.' He goes, 'All right, let's run the numbers.' So, we sat down and did some business modeling projections."

Tana and her husband decided to get into the temp staffing business. One of the three major national staffing firms happened to be headquartered where they were living in Southern California. Tana walked into their offices and eventually met with the CEO, who happened to be looking to add a franchise to his existing operation.

Tana and her husband sold their house in California and moved back to her hometown of Virginia Beach. They took the proceeds of their home sale and used it to set up the first franchisee of the national temp staffing firm. Four years later, they bought a second franchise in Charlotte, a much bigger market. By 2001, they had grown the Charlotte franchise to $15 million in revenue.

In 2002, Tana and her husband created their own staffing company without the overhead of franchise fees. Tana decided she wanted to create a $100 million business, and she hired a senior executive who had taken two companies public to work for her. When he started, he brought with him the idea of staffing for trucking firms. Fifteen years later, Tana had a $64 million business, with half the revenue coming from trucking and half from light manufacturing. Last year, they sold the trucking staffing business.

Tana's survival skills are now finely honed, and today she is executing another major transformation. What's truly extraordinary is that she doesn't have to disrupt her own business.

"We could see the writing on the wall that the staffing industry was broken. It wasn't serving the client or the associates. One hundred and fifty years ago, we came up with the forty-hour work week and everybody worked like that until Uber changed everything. It allowed flexibility. It allowed people to choose their own jobs and became the number one place to work."

Tana believes that if the temp staffing industry doesn't transition to a more flexible staffing model, it will not survive. So she embarked on creating a more tech-enabled firm. She's rebranded her company and is excited about its direction and progress.

"We launched MyWorkChoice a year and a half ago. We have since gone to eight states with large clients—Nordstrom, Shutterfly, Stanley, Fossil, Hot Topic, everywhere where they have large manufacturing or distribution facilities. Ninety-seven-plus percent of our temp staff show up, every day. The workers have dignity because now they can use an app, decide that they can do a Monday morning shift, a Thursday afternoon shift, and a Saturday and a Sunday shift because they can get childcare. Or they're a student and they're in the middle of their midterms, so they can't work for the next two weeks. But hey, they've got a break in a month, and they'll work every shift then.

"We knew we were onto something really big. We put the trucking staffing business up for sale in the beginning of 2018. We ended up closing on that on December 3, 2018, took the proceeds, and put it into this. I think we'll be back up to that $60 million mark soon, so we will have regained everything we sold in the trucking staffing business. We're sitting on a model that's just unbelievable."

> **LESSON LEARNED:** Early life challenges
> give perspective for those later in life.

Tana has forty-three full-time employees, not counting many flex-time workers. Nearly everyone in her call center is flex-time. She has an enormously successful business.

As Tana thinks back on the risks in her life—having a child as a teenager, deciding to survive when she was abused by her first husband, getting married again and moving to California, becoming financially independent, starting a temp staffing franchise, and then creating her own firm and going through two major transformations of the firm. What stands out most is that she didn't view them as risks. She just believed that they would work; she believed in herself. She believes that she connects with others and is a deeply positive person.

Tana didn't take long on our nature versus nurture question—she attributes 100 percent of her success to nature, to how she is wired. She's a born Survivor.

Dan Miller

*"The question is: What are you doing
with your one and only life?"*

Dan Miller grew up in Youngstown, Ohio. His great grandfather started a successful family business, which his dad runs to this day. He was a typical kid in an upper-middle-class Ohio family, a good student, and into sports. He learned early on from his grandfather the importance of treating people with respect and meeting stressful times with equanimity. His grandfather always said to him, "Most people are nice, even if they might not be acting nice at the moment."

Dan was into basketball and tennis when he was growing up. Going into his sophomore year of high school, he was on the junior varsity basketball team. Then, he started noticing he was fatigued all the time. When he told his parents, they thought he might have mononucleosis. He had a blood test done with a pediatrician in town.

His mom, a nurse, used to work in the pediatrician's office where he had the blood test done. One of the nurses at the office called her and told her that something was strange with Dan's blood counts. He went to visit an adult oncologist in Youngstown. At age fourteen, Dan was diagnosed with AML, acute myeloid leukemia. The oncologist urged Dan's parents to go to a pediatric cancer center immediately.

If Dan got any lucky break from this incredibly unlucky scenario, it was that his uncle was a world-renowned pediatric brain tumor specialist who worked at St Jude's Children's Research Hospital in Memphis. Dan's uncle had helped create the Children's Cancer Research Network in the United States. He knew all of the best pediatric oncologists in the country.

Dan's uncle knew the survival rates for pediatric AML were poor, but an experimental new procedure was promising: bone marrow transplants. Dan's uncle connected Dan and his parents with Dr. Beatrice Lampkin at Cincinnati Children's Hospital, who was an early practitioner of bone marrow transplants for pediatric cancer.

The day after the diagnosis, Dan was admitted to Cincinnati Children's Hospital. He was angry—not because his life was suddenly at risk, that was hard for his fourteen-year-old brain to wrap itself around. No, he was angry because he had to leave basketball, tennis, and school, and he knew when he got back to Youngstown, he would be behind in his classes. He also knew he wouldn't see his friends for a good while.

Dr. Lampkin met Dan and his parents in the emergency room. Immediately after introducing herself, she inserted a huge needle into Dan's hip to get a bone marrow sample. Without any sedation. To this day, over thirty years later, Dan remembers how painful that was. She sat down with Dan and his parents and reviewed his results with them in his hospital room:

"You definitely have AML M2. The current five-year survival rate is 25 percent. There's not a lot known about long-term survivors. There are some. The current standard treatment is a chemotherapy regimen called the Denver Protocol. Depending how you respond to that, you may be eligible for a clinical trial with higher doses of chemotherapy and a bone marrow transplant."

Dan is still in touch with Dr. Lampkin over thirty years later. He doesn't think she ever believed the Denver Protocol was going to work. She had to follow that protocol first though, before starting Dan in a bone marrow clinical trial.

"The thing I remember was watching my parents cry. It was very difficult. I remember Dr. Lampkin was telling me a positive attitude makes a big difference, but I was just exhausted. Emotionally, I would say I was overwhelmed, but the way a fourteen-year-old interprets that information is different than how I would interpret it in my forties. When you're fourteen, you don't contemplate death the way a forty-year-old does. I never thought about dying. All I thought about was how terrible it was to see my parents crying. At that point, it's just like, I'm exhausted. I just want to go to sleep, and I'm going to wake up tomorrow, and I'll take on whatever tasks I have to do tomorrow. That was my mindset."

The next nine months were the hardest of Dan's young life. He spent all but one long weekend in the hospital. His mom stayed with him the whole time, sleeping at the Ronald McDonald House or on a little couch in his hospital room. The Denver Protocol of chemo didn't work, and Dr. Lampkin started him on the clinical trial for bone marrow transplantation. The new chemo regimen was brutal. One of the drugs caused Dan to vomit every fifteen minutes for six hours after he got infused, every time, over months.

"That was tough. My blood counts plummeted. I went into the hospital athletic, probably 5'9", 158 pounds, somewhere there, but all muscle. I left nine months later at 120 pounds. I almost died a couple times. I had an allergic reaction to a drug and lost control of my tongue. My jaw locked to the side. I was very sick with infections. I had sepsis on a couple of different occasions when I had literally no white cells in my body. I had fevers of over 104 degrees. They had me on three different antibiotics that weren't working, and they were going to move me to intensive care. Luckily, somehow I survived those things."

After a few months Dan learned he was in remission. But he still faced three major cycles of ablative therapy, where they give you drugs that kill 99 percent of the cells in your body, with the hope that the remaining 1 percent are noncancerous and that you can grow back healthy cells. It pushed him to the edge of life. Back then, the drugs were more primitive. It took two months to recover from each round of ablative therapy.

Dan was emaciated at the end of the nine months, but he was still alive.

At that time, doctors didn't know if the kids who survived the clinical trial needed to go on "maintenance chemo"—regular infusions of the brutal chemo drugs every several months—or if they could just be sent home. When Dr. Lampkin told Dan that the trial might require him to go on maintenance chemo, he asked her some pointed questions. She admitted oncologists didn't know if the maintenance chemo was needed. Dan said, "I'm not doing it. There is no way that you can force me to do it. I've had enough. I'm in remission and I'm done." Years later, research eventually demonstrated that maintenance chemo would have been unnecessary.

Almost dying of cancer is a tough way to find out who your real friends are. Dan remembers returning home to Youngstown:

"I was lucky to have a great circle of friends and a super supportive family. I had friends that kept in touch with me while I was in the hospital. They would come and visit. Before I got sick, I had just started a relationship with Kristen to whom I'm now married. She was really sweet about visiting and keeping in touch with me.

"I went back to loving arms with the help of a big family and lots of friends. One cool thing that happened was that at high school, I was a good student. My parents talked to the principal, and he agreed that if I got some tutoring from some of the teachers in the school on the subjects that I missed, I could stay with my class and start my junior year. That was a pretty cool thing. It would have been hard to start with a class that I didn't know.

"I had some tutoring. The teachers were super nice. I mean, they came, and they did some stuff, but honestly, they just waved me on through. When I started my junior year of high school, I was still emaciated. It took a long time for me to build back up physically, but I was dead set on playing high school basketball—dead set on it.

"The next year, I resumed classes and I started playing basketball. I was able to make my varsity high school basketball team in my senior year. I wasn't a starter, but I was one of the guys off the bench, and we played for the state championship that year. Nobody but me would ever appreciate what it took to come back from where I was, to be able to do that."

Dan learned a lot about risk—and about himself—from this traumatic experience. His idyllic childhood was in many ways over.

"Yeah, I was a different person. I was a good kid beforehand. I had a little more cockiness beforehand, but not arrogance. I mean, I was a good athlete, and I was successful. I felt invincible. Then I went through this horrible experience. I went through a meat grinder for a year and came out an old soul. I faced death and endured serious suffering, serious pain at an early age. There's no way that doesn't change you.

"I had this perspective on 'What is living?' Living is enjoying every day. Living is enjoying your family and your friends, doing good things, doing good deeds. Difficult things happen in everybody's life. Having that perspective about what I went through, it was easier for me to have a bigger life perspective about the little things that come up. That doesn't mean that when my luggage is lost, I don't react the same way anyone else does. It just means I can step away from that easier. Probably, I've always had that advantage."

Dan realized that the essence of life, or at least the essence of his life, was about living and enjoying every day. He realized that difficult things happen to everyone. He began to see that he had a bigger perspective on life.

Dan wanted to become a doctor even before his serious illness. When he was in the hospital, he would sneak up to a higher floor and peer into the window of an operating room during surgery. He decided to get an MD and a PhD in immunology at Ohio State. His girlfriend, Kristen, had moved with him to Columbus, and after a few years they were married. The doctors didn't know if he and Kristen could have children due to all the chemo, but they soon found out she was pregnant.

Dan and Alan met in medical school; Alan realized Dan had a wise perspective on life and wanted to hang out with him. They played basketball together and became fast friends. Alan says, "I always knew he was an old soul. His maturity level was like that of a fifty-year-old man from the moment I met him."

When Dan and his wife had their first daughter, Alyssa, in the middle of the night, Alan was on a shift at the hospital. Alan remembers it like it was yesterday: "I'm on call and there are no cell phones at this time. He paged me when he got to the hospital saying, 'Kris is delivering. We're here.' I was the first non-parent to hold his daughter."

Surviving a life-threatening illness as a young person changed Dan in important ways and changed his view of risk-taking. He suddenly had an old soul—he understood the fragility of life through his very traumatic illness. He learned that every day of life is a gift. But he was also still a young person who had confidence to take risks with his career and life. He took the risk of a high educational investment—getting both a PhD and an MD. He and his wife took the risk of starting a family while he was still in school. After he and Kristen found out she was pregnant, they didn't have the means to support a family, but Dan had the confidence to know they would support each other and make it work. As he puts it, "It was the confidence in knowing my place in the world at a very young age and the confidence to take the risks that I needed to take to follow my path."

> **LESSON LEARNED:** The very act of surviving creates confidence and life perspective.

Dan has continued to create his own life and career. Today, he is an ophthalmologist and retina surgeon at the Cincinnati Eye Institute as well as Chief Medical Officer for CEI Vision Partners, a national ophthalmology company.

Taking risks to Dan was never about being rich or famous; he was simply driven to live the best life he could. For him, that's about doing the things he loves to do and spending time with the people he wants to spend time with. That's what he's done now for a long time. He gets off the path sometimes—just like we all do—but he feels it's easier for him to get back on the path because of what he went through.

Dan sees risk in life as more about time than it is about money. He learned first-hand early on just how precious time is in this life. As he says, "All the other stuff is pointless. The question is, how you are spending your time, with whom, and what are you doing with your one and only life?"

Jennifer Maanavi

"It's going beyond your mental and physical limits. It's self-confidence, it's strength, it's perseverance, it's triumph over challenge."

Jennifer Maanavi grew up in Westchester County, north of New York City. She was an early entrepreneur, starting a cheerleading squad in third grade and selling pom-poms to her fellow cheerleaders. Her mother was a corporate executive at a time when that was a rare career path for women.

For the first two years of college, Jennifer attended Rollins College, a small school in Winter Park, Florida. She made great friends but soon learned she didn't like the heat in Florida and wanted to live in a bigger city. She transferred to Boston University where she finished her degree in English. After graduating she moved to New York City and carved out a career on Wall Street.

Her first job was as a research associate in healthcare and tech for a family-owned investment firm. She started taking finance classes at night to learn more about accounting and the securities industry. After a few years, Jennifer landed a job as a salesperson at Prudential in what would be called a hedge fund today. Prudential paid for her to get an MBA at Columbia Business School in a two-year weekend program.

"I graduated on a Sunday, and I was literally going to have the same job Monday that I had on Friday," Jennifer explains. "That seemed anti-climactic. It was a heavily commission-based role, and you don't necessarily make more money just because you have your MBA. It wasn't exciting for me to stay in the job even though I liked it. So, that's when I left." Prudential could have come after her for tuition, which was $90,000, but they never did.

Jennifer found a job at Morgan Stanley, where she stayed from 1998 to 2003. She loved the transactional part of Wall Street; even today, with her own business that she's run for fourteen years, she gets excited when the phone rings. She left Wall Street because she learned the hard way that Wall Street back then was not supportive of young mothers.

"The leaving was unfortunate. And I know this isn't a story about women on Wall Street, but it was unfortunate. The thing that made me walk out the door was a disappointing conversation with my manager. We worked in an open office environment, so people can hear you on the phone. My son was six months old and was sick, so I was on the phone with my pediatrician.

"My manager, whom I'd known for five years, who also had two children at home and a Harvard Law School wife who chose not to work, said to me, 'I hope these phone calls to the pediatrician don't keep up. How many of these types of phone calls do you think we'll be having?' I thought, *Oh my God, I am absolutely never working here again.* That's really all you have to do to a new mom to piss her off for the rest of her life. It was one of those moments."

Jennifer faced an emotional survival issue. Not physical survival like Dan, or domestic abuse like Tana, but having a child was an issue that came up frequently in our interviews with women. Her physical and financial health were fine. Her husband was also working on Wall Street and doing well financially. Yet, by having a child, her professional environment became unsupportive. Like most people on Wall Street, she was frequently working from 7:00 a.m. until 7.30 p.m., which were the only hours when her child was awake.

Jennifer knew she didn't want a life of being at work early in the morning, traveling away from her kids, and being on corporate conference calls on Sunday afternoons. She knew she needed to make a change. Once she left her career track on Wall Street in her mid-thirties, there would be no turning back.

When she was a child, Jennifer loved dance. As an adult she attended a regular dance-based exercise class at a fitness studio in Manhattan. As she contemplated her professional future, the fitness studio abruptly shut down.

"I had been attending this class three or four times a week for many years," Jennifer recalls. "While in the back of my head I'm thinking my banking career might be coming to an end, that particular exercise studio that I adored closed." The landlord decided to repurpose the building, and the owner of the studio was in her mid-sixties, so she decided to close the doors. "After a couple of days, I thought, *You know what, I should figure out what's going on here, because this is such a good mix of my interest in fitness, my background in dance, banking and finance experience, my MBA. This could be a great opportunity for me.* I didn't necessarily have any idea how much money you could make running a fitness studio. That wasn't what this was about. It was more like, *Oh, this is just a great blend of my talents, and hopefully some flexibility*, which I was looking for." Jennifer quit her job and contacted the landlord.

> **LESSON LEARNED:** Risk-takers often take a
> circuitous route back to their original passions.

Jennifer is scrappy when it comes to structuring new opportunities. She learned that way back when she was selling pompoms to fellow cheerleaders in the third grade. On the day that the fitness studio closed, she ran into pockets of women outside crying because they were so upset. She took that as a positive sign of market demand and began taking down phone numbers of crying women that she hardly knew. She then reached out to Tanya, the best instructor at the now-closed fitness studio, to see if she wanted to partner with her. Tanya thought she was crazy. When she finally agreed to meet, Jennifer showed up to the coffee shop with a business plan to build a new fitness studio. Jennifer and Tanya have been partners ever since.

After a few months borrowing space in other locations, Jennifer signed a ten-year lease to rent a studio on the eighth floor of an art gallery. She branded her studio Physique 57 and opened her new location on February 6, 2006. Jennifer and Tanya had thirty-two paying customers on the first day. They started with forty classes a week and three instructors.

Jennifer concentrated on branding and positioning, which were critical in a fitness industry that was in its infancy. Her classes were marketed as barre fitness classes before the term was widely used.

"I really focused on the target market. I wanted a younger demographic. I offered special pricing for the twenty-seven-and-under crowd. And I just got better at it. Originally, my goal was just to get this place open and get our former clients back in. Then I really started thinking about how to market it. Next thing I knew, we were in *Vogue* magazine. Sarah Jessica Parker started to come. It really started to take off."

Jennifer and Tanya worked every single day for the first two years. Within a year of opening, they opened a new studio in the

Hamptons and another in Manhattan. The business was profitable in the first year; Jennifer poured all of the profits into building out studios, hiring instructors, and marketing. She worked hard, but she never took external investment money, and she never had to get on a Sunday afternoon conference call. She now has three children.

Jennifer understands the good fortune involved in her success.

"We hit the market at an amazing time. Women had nowhere to go. Gyms were mostly geared for men. Yoga studios were sort of hippie. Pilates studios were considered boring. I targeted twenty-eight-year-old women. I hired this fashion PR firm because I wanted this to be considered a fashionable thing to do, more so than fitness, and I turned it into a different type of lifestyle and community, geared toward affluent, trendy younger women. That was the key to our success."

Physique 57 grew to 430 classes a week in New York alone, with additional studios in Dubai, Bangkok, Mumbai, and Manila. Jennifer started franchising studios in the United States.

Jennifer started Physique 57 before it became fashionable to have mission statements for every business, but she feels the mission deep in her bones. She quoted a line from her company's manifesto: "We thrive on equal parts unshakable strength and unbreakable faith, and in feeling strong, seen, and worthwhile every day."

She makes it clear that she has a mission beyond profits. "I really want to make a dent in the universe, and I knew from my experience with exercise that it transformed me from the inside out. It's so much more than exercise for me. It's going beyond your mental and physical limits. It's self-confidence, it's strength, it's perseverance, it's triumph over challenge. That's how I look at fitness. Yes, sure, you look nice in jeans, but there's so much more to it."

There is no perfect time for risk-taking.

Robin, Tana, and Dan could have never anticipated the events that transformed their lives. Finding out that your life savings are gone because your spouse has a hidden addiction, that your new teenage husband is abusive, that you have leukemia when you are fourteen years old—these are not normal routine life events. Jennifer understood that Wall Street wasn't a great workplace in the early 2000s for young working mothers, but she still had to invent a career out of thin air.

What's notable about these life survival events is how they increased the confidence level of the risk-taker. Instead of becoming paralyzed by the challenges, Robin, Tana, Dan, and Jennifer felt more confidence to deal with whatever challenges they faced next. It's as if staring into the abyss freed them to take more risk, rather than less.

Not surprisingly, the Survivors as a group demonstrated Livewith Two: Head and Heart more strongly than any other category of risk-takers. The events of their lives forced them to reflect deeply and with high emotional intelligence on their mission and purpose.

CHAPTER EIGHT

Seekers

As we've seen, money is often not enough. Everyone wants to find meaning in their life, and that quest for meaning can take a lifetime.

Nikola Tesla was a Seeker his entire life. At twenty-eight years old in 1884, he immigrated to the United States with four cents in his pocket.

Tesla worked for a division of Thomas Edison's company in Paris and secured a similar position in the United States when he arrived. Edison was an inventor focused on practical applications. Tesla sought to unravel the mysteries of electricity, not create the next electrical appliance. He lasted six months at Edison.

Soon after leaving, Tesla achieved a breakthrough, inventing the AC (alternating current) power format still in use today. It was a brilliant innovation, but Tesla needed the help of George Westinghouse to commercialize it.

In 1888, the Westinghouse Corporation bought Tesla's AC power inventions for $60,000, a $2,000 annual retainer, and a $2.50 licensing fee for every horsepower of AC used. Three years later, Westinghouse was facing defaults on bank loans and informed Tesla they could no longer afford his licensing fee.

Tesla released George Westinghouse from the deal. He didn't want to bother with growing the business of his brilliant invention because he was confident he could invent the next big thing, probably before breakfast the next morning.

Westinghouse paid Tesla $216,000 for all the rights to AC power. He was now both rich and famous and in a fantastic position to raise money for his many creative inventions. However, like many Seekers, he was unconcerned with personal wealth and oblivious to investors' desire to seek financial returns.

The vision that most captivated Tesla was cheap, wireless, worldwide electric power. His invention of AC power for long-distance electric transmission, and its subsequent use for electric power at Niagara Falls, had given him the credibility he needed.

In 1899, Tesla built a laboratory in Colorado Springs designed to realize his visions. He said at the time, "The day when we shall know exactly what 'electricity' is, will chronicle an event probably greater, more important than any other recorded in the history of the human race. The time will come when the comfort, the very existence, perhaps, of man will depend upon that wonderful agent."[14]

His financial benefactor, John Jacob Astor, was in Europe at the time and unaware of Tesla's move to Colorado Springs. Despite frenetic experimentation, Tesla failed to produce anything of commercial value during the next seven months and returned to New York City.

Tesla continued his efforts to create a wireless electrical transmission system, and in 1901 he raised $150,000 (over $4.5 million in today's dollars) from JP Morgan; Tesla mesmerized him with charismatic product demonstrations emulated years later by Apple cofounder Steve Jobs. He built a large electric facility on Long Island, but by 1915 he lost the property in foreclosure.

Tesla never stopped seeking risk. His biographers have credited him with inventing the induction motor, the electric power distribution system, fluorescent and neon lighting, wireless communication, remote control, and robotics. To a large degree, one hundred years later, we live in the world that Tesla envisioned.

But Tesla was a Seeker, one who never concerned himself with commercializing his creations. He lived in his mind, which lived in the future. He once said, "The scientific man does not aim at an immediate result. He does not expect that his advanced ideas will be readily taken up. His work is like that of the planter—for the future. His duty is to lay the foundation for those who are to come and point the way."[15]

Many risk-takers learn the limits of external rewards, especially after they have acquired some. They discover that what they really want to do is to "find themselves." This can involve just as much risk-taking, if not more, as chasing material rewards and external accolades.

These risk-takers come to fully understand Livewith Five: Risk Tastes Different with Age.

Jim Fallon

"Again, here I was faced with a big decision. But this time,
I decided to not take the job and move to a new place."

Jim Fallon grew up in Champaign, Illinois, and attended college
at the University of Wisconsin at Madison. He started out being a
math and physics major, but he found himself drawn to philosophy.
He double majored in philosophy and psychology.

"I was curious about the existential questions of life," Jim says.
"Even as a young kid, I was puzzling over life questions like, where
is the edge of the universe, and what will be the fate of the human
race? I was a Catholic school kid. I used to pray for the answers
to those questions.

"I saw my dad being an entrepreneur, so I'd always thought I'd
do something like that. I had a lawn-mowing business at one point.
I took a job at a grocery store, and it lasted about three days. I
thought, *No way. Is this going to be my life?* But when I was in college,
I tuned into who I was as a person, and started exploring those
more existential questions, such as, *Do we have free will?"*

After college, Jim went back to his hometown and took a job
with a software company called Wolfram Research. The company
was growing fast, and he quickly moved up the ranks. After a year
in Illinois, they asked him to move to Oxford, England, to start a
European operation for the company. He was twenty-two years
old. Wolfram developed a programming language, still in existence,
which enabled powerful mathematical computations on several
computing platforms. Jim stayed there four years. He understood
the product well, but he was more interested in business strategy.

After he left Wolfram, Jim went to the University of Texas in

Austin to get an MBA. By then he was pretty sure that he wanted to start his own software company.

Jim spent the better part of the next fifteen years balancing his rational, logical mind with the more intuitive decision-making entrepreneurs often follow. He started out right after his MBA working for the Boston Consulting Group, a premier strategy consulting firm. Jim loved the work, which he thought of as "philosophy for business." However, after two years there, Jim's drive to get involved in software start-ups became overwhelming. It was the late 1990s and the dot-com boom was really taking off. He got involved with two organizations that were trying to create "electronic marketplaces," which were all the rage back then.

The first e-marketplace company Jim got involved with was in Dallas and was focused on the insurance industry. The second was in Baltimore, and the company created an e-marketplace for the apparel industry supply chain. Neither company survived the dot-com crash of 2001, but Jim made some money along the way and learned a lot about how to launch a software company. Most importantly, he also met his wife in Baltimore.

LESSON LEARNED: Risk-takers treat opportunities like surfers treat waves—there's always another one.

After they married, Jim took on a company turnaround in San Diego with an electronics manufacturer that was heavily in debt to its Chinese suppliers. As the business was starting to turn around, he met someone with an idea for a biotech company. Jim loved the product idea, and his research found that it was a multi-billion-dollar market opportunity. But he had a wife and a newborn son, and the new company could be out of cash in eighteen months.

After some soul-searching, he decided to take the leap into the biotech firm, which he and his partner launched in early 2006. They had no customers and only a prototype product. His wife was totally supportive of taking the risk.

The biotech firm, called Innovive, got off to a great start. Even while they were still in preclinical research, they had an offer in 2008 from a larger pharma firm to buy the company for $35 million in cash plus $100 million in earn-outs. But the market crash of 2008 changed everything—especially the valuation of early-stage biotech firms. The deal fell apart and Jim and his partner realized they had to grind it out and build the business. The headquarters was in San Diego, but most of their customers were on the East Coast. They decided to relocate their headquarters, and Jim and his family moved to Boston in 2013.

Jim's career followed a steady trajectory from 2003 to 2015. It was in many ways a well-worn path—work for a few years, go to business school for an MBA, take a job with a strategy consulting firm, then embark on a career in progressively more interesting start-ups with progressively increasing responsibilities. In Howard Gardner's multiple intelligences framework, Jim had until this point relied on his *logical/mathematical intelligence.*

In 2015 Jim's life took an unexpected turn. Still in his forties, he was diagnosed with prostate cancer.

"It was a surreal experience, for sure. Leaving the business was scary. What I remember most is thinking, *How do I let go of my equity and take care of my health?* In the end, we worked out a deal that meant I didn't have to worry about working for a few years."

After Jim negotiated his exit and some financial breathing room, he underwent surgery in 2016. The surgery went well, but he would still need to be tested periodically for the next ten years. Two years after the surgery, there was no sign of cancer.

For the first time in his adult life, Jim had time to reflect. He realized he had been moving through life at an incredibly fast pace. He came to understand that he needed to be more self-aware of what really mattered in his life.

During his ten years at Innovive, Jim lost fifty pounds and began eating healthily. Exercise became a regular part of his routine. Then he picked up a meditation practice. He began using his time off to take some courses on introspection to better understand the meaning of life.

"Somewhere in the middle of 2016, I woke up and realized that I'd been chasing these future outcomes my whole life and hadn't been appreciating the journey that I was on. I know it sounds cliché, but suddenly I realized all I really wanted to do was be of service, however I could. For the first time, I envisioned doing different kinds of work.

"Around the same time, the executive vice president of the company that almost acquired Innovive in 2008 called me and asked if he could put my name in a hat for a CEO role that was coming up in the industry. I said, 'Sure,' even though I'd said I wouldn't work for a year. I had a totally different perspective as I went through the interview process on my orientation to life.

"The job I was offered was perfect. The company was a bit bigger than Innovive and had been bought by a private equity company. They wanted to double the revenue over the next five years. It was everything that I had described that I wanted for my next gig. Here I was faced with a big decision. I decided to not take the job and move to a new place. I was going to stick with what was unfolding. I felt like I needed more time. That was in the middle of 2016.

"My decision-making processes were shifting. The sense of urgency I'd had my whole life had faded. I was beginning to appreciate that decisions can percolate, especially big decisions that are going to change the course of your life. It could percolate for a longer period of time, and there may be greater wisdom that comes through from that. I could let go of being attached to whatever."

Life just didn't look the same to Jim after his cancer diagnosis, his process of stepping back to gain more perspective, and his recovery. Even though he knew that if he took the CEO position he would likely never have to work again, he turned it down. He just didn't want *that* kind of job anymore. He wanted to develop his introspection skills and *intrapersonal intelligence,* not just his logical intelligence.

> **LESSON LEARNED:** Risk-takers often say "no"
> to conventional rewards to clarify their goals.

Jim decided his life mission was less about running companies and more about helping other executives with their own mindfulness and emotional intelligence journeys. While there were clues like the decision to major in philosophy and psychology in college, there was nothing in his professional trajectory that would have suggested such a decision. Jim had survived one of life's most challenging events, a cancer diagnosis, and he was ready for a new kind of life.

In 2016, he was getting coaching himself to help determine his next step. His coach sent him an email recommending that he coach someone else. He thought about it and realized he was interested. Then he went through an intense six-month coaching certification process with New Ventures West.

His coaching work and training made him think profoundly about a concept called "Whole Body Yes." Using Whole Body Yes, you don't just listen to your rational, logical mind, but you listen to your Whole Body when making life decisions.

Jim began to realize the power of seeking a Whole Body Yes:

"Going into 2017, I was noticing that all the commitments I added to my calendar around Whole Body Yes were so much fun. I was starting to get the sense that I didn't have a Whole Body Yes to being in another start-up. It was actually draining my energy.

"So, I made another financial decision. I wasn't going to do start-ups anymore. I was letting go of whatever future financial potential that business was going to have. It felt really clean.

"If you draw a two-by-two, with the vertical axis being how good are you at something, and the horizontal axis being how much you love it, what I find in corporate America are so many people are in the upper left-hand corner. They're really good at it but they don't love it. There are so many smart people who are doing jobs that they just don't like. They are the ones that have midlife crises.

"It explains why people wake up in their forties and say, 'God, I can't believe I've been doing this thing for so long.' You get more money, you get more positive strokes, you get better titles. You impress people because you're smart and you're good at it, but it drains your energy over time.

"I lived that life. I lived in the upper left-hand corner, running these software companies, and doing these things. And then, as I used this Whole Body Yes process, at first, I felt like, *Wow, I'm never going to get anything on my calendar. It's like a big void.* And then, at the end of 2017, I realized my calendar was totally full and I loved all of it. It was unfolding beautifully. And that just seemed to happen."

> ### KEY CONCEPT—LIFE FULFILLMENT MAXIMIZATION:
> You live a fulfilling life by marrying what you are good at with what you love to do.

Looking back, Jim has taken all kinds of risks: when he left BCG to get involved in start-ups, when he left a secure job in San Diego to move into biotech, when he moved back to the East Coast to run that biotech firm, and many more. But everything changed when he was diagnosed with prostate cancer. He began to live a more conscious life, and more of a life of service to his family and other leaders.

Jim's experience is that by continuing to take risks, and especially to take the risk of looking at his own life, he finally found himself. Today he lives in Boulder, Colorado, where he is a leadership and executive coach, working with The Conscious Leadership Group. Jim's primary focus is helping CEOs develop greater self-awareness and emotional intelligence. He finds that whatever the issue of the day is for a particular leader, addressing the issue almost always requires more self-awareness.

Peter Denning

"Something had been triggered in him, finally. He hugged his parents and told them he loved them. And then he left."

Peter Denning grew up in Fort Worth as the seventh of eleven children. His dad created a successful family business, still in existence, which sells petroleum-based lubricants used in industrial processes all over the world.

Peter grew up in a life of privilege, even though he didn't fully realize how well off his family was. With eleven kids, everything was organized and regimented.

Peter soon had everything in life that most people want—money, a career of achievement, a great family, a beautiful home, a robust social life. But, in the end, Peter's story isn't about that. It's about the one thing that he didn't have—a fulfilling inner life—and what he had to risk to get it.

Peter's father was his role model. From very early in his life, his father wanted him to join the family business, as his older brothers had done. After attending a private high school, Peter went to the University of Texas at Austin and earned an economics degree. His dad wanted him to start work immediately upon graduation. Instead, Peter bought a one-way ticket to New York City, found a job working on Wall Street, and sold suits at Brooks Brothers on Madison Avenue on the nights and weekends.

His dad didn't talk to him for the next six months. After three years in New York, Peter moved back to Texas, but he took a job in Dallas instead. Then, after three or four years, his dad fell sick with a heart condition. He still wanted Peter to join the family business and sent Peter's brothers to talk to him.

Finally, Peter relented. He wanted to gain some international business experience, so he took a job running the plant for the family business's European subsidiary in Antwerp, Belgium. He married his wife right before the move; their first house was in Antwerp.

Peter and his wife had a great four years in Belgium. He believes that the times in his life when he took the greatest risks were also the times when he felt the most alive. It happened when he bought the one-way ticket to New York after graduating, and it happened again in Belgium. It was about Peter finding his own way, rather than having it all handed to him. Still, he knew early on there was always a safety net waiting for him back in Texas.

Peter turned the plant around in Belgium, traveling all over Europe for the business. After four years, his wife was homesick for Texas, and his dad wanted him to come back and take over the whole company. He moved back to Fort Worth, for the first time since leaving for college, and started working out of headquarters. He was thirty-five years old.

Peter ran one of the company's divisions successfully in the late 1990s, but he began to get tired of the company politics. He felt that some of the key people in the business, nonfamily members, were not good for the business. He was ready to leave, but after 9/11 his dad talked him into staying and asked him to run another major division of the company, the lubricant division, which was not performing well. For the next twelve years, Peter led the lubricant division to ten straight years of revenue growth and significant profitability improvement. He expanded the product lines and hired over a thousand new sales reps. They moved into new markets and were soon firing on all cylinders. It was a great success, which Peter had pulled off in a risk-averse family business with limited resources.

There's this thing about climbing a mountain. It shows up in many of our interviews. Once you reach the top of the mountain, you think you will feel gratified. But many successful people experience an anticlimactic feeling of emptiness. They realize there is more to life than the mountain you just climbed, even if it was really hard.

> **KEY CONCEPT—INNER FULFILLMENT**
> **RISK:** When people have everything they need, materially, they often experience emptiness and must take more risks for inner fulfillment.

Peter began searching for what else to do with his life. The business was doing well. He had a beautiful "forever" home in Fort Worth, and in many ways he had an idyllic life. But he was looking for something more than that. Peter asked himself some fundamental questions. What did he really want? What was his life about? How was he doing with the most important relationships in his life? By this time, Peter and his wife had three children, and like many fathers, he felt he didn't see his kids enough.

He went on a retreat in Australia for a week. On the eighteen-hour flight home he wrote twenty pages of notes to himself.

"It was a fundamental turning point for me. I knew exactly what I wanted. I wanted my family. I wanted this epic family adventure. I wanted twelve months minimum abroad exploring the world. I had this motivating vision of creating deep connections, unbreakable bonds, with all the adventures we were going to do together. It would broaden them. It would make them world travelers. It would make them chart their own courses. I was ready to make it happen.

"From the time I got back from Australia and talked to my wife, she was on board. She said, 'Where should we go?' We kicked it around for a week or two. I woke up one day from sleeping by the pool and I said, 'It's Spain. It's Spain, the most family-focused, relaxed, simple life.' My wife and I had been there, and I loved Barcelona. It's one of my favorite cities in the world. I got tickets within three weeks. The five of us were on a flight to Madrid, Barcelona, Valencia. We were going to explore, look at houses, look at schools, connect with the locals."

It was March of 2015. Peter's family held a weekly family meeting. At the next family meeting, the topic was to vote whether or not to go to Spain for a year. Everyone wanted to go. Peter started working on the logistics of leaving the country for a year—passports, visas, even a trip to the Spanish embassy in Dallas. Three weeks after that trip to the embassy, all five members of the family had their visas approved to go to Spain for a year.

There was one issue, of course, and it was a big one.

Peter had to talk to his dad and tell him he was leaving the company to spend a year in Spain. His dad hardly ever even took a week's vacation. Initially, his dad was excited for Peter and his family. He was flabbergasted that he would make such a decision. He tried to talk Peter into taking a sabbatical, but Peter needed a clean break. He was quitting, even if his dad didn't yet believe that.

Peter and his family got rid of everything. They sold their house to a friend who made a fair offer and gave away the rest. Trucks from different charities came through the circular drive at Peter's large house in Fort Worth and took the appliances, clothes, furniture—everything. Friends told them they were crazy and asked repeatedly why they were doing this.

The family emptied their 5,000-square-foot house of all the

possessions they had worked so hard to get except for a small storage unit for sentimental items. They were each taking only one suitcase to Spain. It wasn't all easy. Peter's wife grew up middle-class, and she hung onto things. She cried, but in the end, she jumped into their new life. On the day they left for the airport, Peter handed the keys to his Jaguar, which he loved, to a neighbor who had always admired the car.

> **LESSON LEARNED:** Risk-takers often need a clean break from "safety" to achieve perspective.

They left for Spain in July 2015, four months after they had decided to go. They didn't have any keys left to anything and didn't need any. All they had was one another and five suitcases. They had signed a lease to rent a house in Valencia for a year.

They did have money; Peter figured enough for at least ten years before he would have to work again. They weren't risking material needs, but they were risking their whole lives they built in Fort Worth. Peter was walking away from everything he built at the company. He was no longer a big-shot business guy.

Valencia is a beautiful, bucolic city. The kids only had to walk 200 meters to get to school. Their house was a couple of miles from the beach. They were spending time together as a family in ways they couldn't in Fort Worth.

"I would say honestly, as I was going through this time and decompressing and trying to get clear, everything became more vivid," Peter recalls. "The sights, the smells, everything. I became joyful again. It was truly the happiest I'd been, maybe since I was a kid."

Peter realized this time together with his family was about finding himself and figuring out what he wanted from life. He was nearing fifty years old, and he had lived his whole life in the shadow of his talented and often controlling father. Peter had accomplished amazing things, but it was still his father's business, and that was never going to change. Peter had constantly sought and craved approval from his father, never wanting to disappoint him. Maybe that was what needed to change.

"I was afraid of losing my identity. The performance paradox is that everything that has got me here—the title, the money, the prestige—why in the world would I let that go? Why would I walk away from that? The truth was that I was afraid. I was afraid of losing me, of losing all this stuff, but that was exactly what was keeping me from going where I needed to go. I knew that. It was time for me to step into the unknown."

That period in Valencia was almost too good to be true. As it tends to do, life soon grew more complicated for Peter. Occasionally, he traveled on his own back to Texas. On one such trip, his parents asked him to stop by. When he arrived, his father was angry. They just didn't understand why he would leave it all behind. His father told him, "There's a huge hole in the business with you not here." It was as if his father was dealing with the death of his loyal son Peter.

So much of our lives are about expectations—what others expect of us, what we expect of ourselves. Peter realized he had been living his life to fulfill his father's expectations; he had given the family business everything for so many years. In a moment of clarity he knew it was never going to be enough. He would never fulfill his dad's expectations, no matter what he did.

After listening to his parents for more than four hours, Peter got up from the dining room table. There was a long, uncomfortable silence, and then he hugged them. Something had been triggered in him, finally. He had the deep sensation that he was floating above the room—in the room, but not of it. He told his parents that he loved them. And then he left.

He didn't speak to them again for nine months.

> **LESSON LEARNED:** Seeking fulfillment
> in the unknown is the first risk.

Peter was fifty years old when this happened, and his dad was eighty-five. Peter had just become a man. He wasn't going to live his life for his parents anymore. What they wanted from him and what he wanted for himself and his own family were not the same. It was that fundamental. He loved them deeply, but he had to find himself.

He flew back to Spain. Everything was the same on the outside, but inside Peter, everything was different. He no longer needed anyone's approval to live his own life.

Peter is a Type 1 diabetic. He realized, acutely, vividly, that he only has so much time left on this planet. He was going to live his life on his own terms.

He took more risks—not for money but for joy. He traveled and had incredible adventures with his family in Europe. He'd run half marathons, but in the next year he ran three full marathons. He developed deep, fierce bonds with his sons. Peter and his family decided to spend a second year in Valencia.

After nine months, Peter knew he needed to talk to his parents. They were in their mid-eighties, and it was immature not to talk. He called them and told them he loved them, that everything was great on his end. They were gracious. Sometimes during conflict, the words "I love you" make an enormous difference. Both Peter and his parents said those three words to each other.

After two years in Spain, the family took another vote. Peter and his wife both wanted to stay, but two of his three sons were ready to come home. Without a unanimous vote, it was time to come home. When they landed back in Texas, they had no home and few possessions. They stayed with his parents for ten days. Peter's dad still wanted him to return to the business, but he was past that point. He couldn't do it.

Since returning home from Spain, Peter and his family have opted for a simpler life.

"Essentially, I transformed my business life and my personal life. The life that's simple, Spanish life, living with nothing and not acquiring, that is the life we're committed to keeping. We don't require anything. We don't need anything. This is what this time has taught us. The boys, they don't need anything for Christmas. On my birthday, they washed the car, the one car. We live outside of Dallas in an old ranch with concrete floors, on a couple acres north of town. I had a mattress on the floor for nine months, with cardboard boxes, not even taped up, as side tables. We bought a TV and a couch, and we're happy. We finally got a second car, even though we have four drivers. We're just committed to living this life.

"I believe that if you're awake to it, every connection has a purpose. It's up to you to find why. And I can tell you all day every day I'm faced with these unbelievable connections stirring through my life. I take the time to talk to people, and I look and try to see inside them wondering what I could do to serve that person? What could I uniquely do? What small thing could help make them feel like they are a hero?"

Peter mostly works with family businesses these days, sharing what he has learned, helping where he can, and honoring their journey.

Sue Chen

"I was not put on this earth to be a bystander. I can't deny that. I am a force. Whether I like it or not, I am."

Sue Chen was born in Taiwan and immigrated to the United States in 1973 when she was three years old. Her family started out in Brooklyn, New York. Her father, who was a rehabilitation doctor, came to the United States a few years earlier, before they received the immigration papers for the rest of the family.

Sue had never seen non-Asian people until she got to the United States. She had also never had ice cream—to this day she still loves ice cream.

Her father did his residency as a rehab doctor at Temple University in Philadelphia. He had already been a doctor in Taiwan, but he had to start over in the United States, working for the Veterans Administration. After graduating from Temple, the family moved to Dublin, Georgia, a rural community with a large VA hospital. Sue was seven years old; she didn't really understand racism at that age, but she definitely remembers being called names.

Sue's father was focused on healing veterans, and he was compassionate and innovative in his approach to healing. She recalls visiting him at the hospital, and being inspired by the kind of doctor he was, how much of a difference he made in the lives of disabled veterans.

Sue's father had a slow growing form of cancer from the time he immigrated to the United States. He knew he would not live long, and he had a wife and three young daughters to support. He wanted to give his family a more idyllic place to live before he died, so he moved jobs to a hospital in Davie, Florida, and bought a farm. They had a few acres with chickens, ducks, and cows. Her father was an avid tennis player, and a huge admirer of Arthur Ashe, the great African American tennis player who later died of AIDS following a blood transfusion for heart disease. Sue's dad built a tennis court on their small property and taught his daughters how to play. The property was his dream.

When Sue was twelve, her dad began to talk to her about dating and marriage. She was barely entering puberty and thought the conversations were awkward and odd. She soon learned the cancer had spread to his liver, and he was engaging in these conversations because he knew he didn't have much time left. Her father died when Sue was fourteen years old.

> **LESSON LEARNED:** Tragic life
> circumstances can shape risk-taker choices.

Sue, her mom, and her two sisters were now alone in rural Florida. Sue and her older sister were doing well in school, so her mom endured the loneliness and stayed in Florida until Sue graduated from high school. After that, the family moved to LA where there was a support network of Taiwanese immigrants.

Sue got through the pain of her father's illness and death by keeping busy in high school, which she now realizes began a life-long pattern of using busyness to manage emotional pain.

Sue needed financial support to make it through college, and she got a full scholarship at Trinity University, a small college in

San Antonio. By her own assessment, Sue was an average student. She wasn't sure what to do afterward, so she moved back to LA and lived with her mom, and took an entry-level marketing job.

When he was still alive, Sue's dad had started a manufacturing company in Taiwan to make rehab medical devices for distribution in America. He never worked in the company full time, but he had gotten one of his brothers involved. Now, nearly ten years after her father's death, two of Sue's uncles and her grandfather were still trying to get the company off the ground. Their problem wasn't the products being manufactured in Taiwan—it was finding the right distribution partner in the States.

About a year after Sue graduated, her uncles and grandfather asked her to attend a meeting in San Francisco with a potential distribution partner. They wanted Sue's help in reviewing a thirty-eight-page legal contract. She wasn't a lawyer, but she had a college degree and wasn't afraid. She spent a few hours with everyone, including the potential partners, asking questions. She concluded the contract was totally one-sided and told her uncles and grand-father not to sign it.

Sue's grandfather was strong, patriarchal, and believed in family. He turned to Sue and said, "You're going to start a company to distribute our products. You're going to do this out of respect for your father." Her uncles told her grandfather that she didn't have the experience to do this, but he insisted that she start a company, and that the uncles would support her.

This was Sue's Moment of Truth. She agreed to start the company. She had been dreaming of doing something big; she didn't want to spend her life buried in some large organization. She was only twenty-three years old, with virtually no business experience, but she had courage and a desire to do something meaningful and valuable with her life. She had no idea how to set up a business corporation, let alone run one, but she said yes anyway, and Nova Medical Products was born.

> **LESSON LEARNED:** Risk-takers often need purpose like regular people need air.

Not surprisingly, the early days of the business were difficult.

"It didn't blow up, thank God," she says. "My uncles gave me $200,000 in capital to start and $200,000 in inventory, so I had $400,000, and then they said, 'That's it. That's all we've got.' It was tough because the product is sold through medical dealer providers, these old mom-and-pop shops that bill Medicare for walkers and crutches. You're not really selling anything of value. It's just a commodity. I shopped around the product, going to medical supply stores to get them to use it. Why would they? It was tough.

"We sat on a bunch of crutches and canes and walkers. And then my uncle said, 'In Europe, they developed this different type of sporty walker. It has wheels and brakes. You want to bring some in?' I said, 'Sure, it's something different.' I brought some in, and there wasn't a Medicare code on it, so I couldn't sell it. But it was a cool product. We would try it on a couple of people, and they'd say, 'Wow, I can actually walk and sit. That's pretty cool.'

"Since we couldn't sell it, we ended up giving away a hundred of them. I went to UCLA's rehab department where I used to visit my dad. The therapists were super nice and always wanted to find ways to help their patients. I'd visit them and drop off these walkers. Eventually, they said, 'Hey, how can I get these for my patients?' At the same time, there was a code on Medicare that described a walker with a seat. If you wrote the prescription right, you could get it paid for. That really saved us. Thank God, we had this Medicare code. We took it all the way to the bank. And then, Medicare decided, 'Hey, too many people were billing for these fancy walkers. Let's kill it.'

"But people loved the product. I thought, *Why don't we try to sell it in a retail store?* We made a retail box. I got a couple of models and did a photo shoot and tried to sell it in a box. It was hard. We took a lot of risk in the beginning guaranteeing the sale and full return in retail stores, but it worked."

Sue started the business in the early 1990s, and she spent a few years understanding the relationship between the mom-and-pop stores that were distributing her products and the Medicare agency. It was not a healthy relationship. Medicare made all the rules and the mom-and-pop stores needed to comply. Medicare didn't support any kind of product innovation; they viewed the Medicare population as elderly and disabled. The only color walker they reimbursed for was grey. The Medicare relationship with mom-and-pop distributors was dysfunctional.

Sue felt her business would be stronger with a more direct relationship with customers. She wanted to cultivate that. She decided to put an 800 number on their wheelchairs and canes and walkers, so that the customer could call Nova if there were a problem. Soon after that, a lady called to get her walker fixed. She was local, so she came to the office. Sue started chatting with her and asked what color she would want in a walker and she said "red" because she was a "hot, sexy grandma."

Sue loved adding style to medical equipment. But Medicare didn't reimburse for it.

She decided Medicare was too difficult to deal with and made an unheard of decision. She cut ties with Medicare and started training her mom-and-pop store customers to be retailers rather than Medicare providers. Her business began to grow. It turned out there were plenty of people who were willing to pay for red walkers, or canes with leopard-print handles.

> **LESSON LEARNED:** Entrepreneurial risk-takers often take unconventional paths to reach their customers.

Nova Medical Products was still growing fast ten years in, but Sue was not.

She got married in 2006. Her husband developed a gambling problem and the relationship soon turned abusive. When her marriage started crumbling, Sue began taking scuba diving trips and saw a few sharks up close. One night she dreamed about the beautiful sharks and the suffering they endured. She did some research and realized they were an endangered species due to the inhumane slaughter of sharks for shark fin soup. Legislation banned shark finning and distribution of shark fin, but unfortunately, there was an Asian shark trade that hired lobbyists and had no interest in shark preservation and conservation.

Sue got involved in a shark conservation nonprofit based in New York, sending them a $5,000 check to rebuild their website. The shark conservation effort had nothing to do with her business, Nova, but it felt important to her. Working on it made her feel alive and distracted her from thinking about her abusive husband or crumbling marriage.

Sue then volunteered with a California-based nonprofit called Reef Check. One day, she was on a conference call with every ocean and animal advocate group in the state, and someone said she should be their spokesperson. There was supportive legislation picking up steam in California, but also support for the Asian shark trade that wanted to kill the bill.

Sue agreed to be the spokesperson and began spending more time in Sacramento. She was worried that her team at Nova Medical Products would feel like she was spending too much time on these conservation efforts, but she had a supportive team at work, and they were understanding.

Eventually, thanks to Sue's communication efforts, the shark conservation bill passed. Sue found her voice during this turbulent time in her life.

"I've had many years and discussions reflecting on this. I was going through so much else in my life. I would wake up every day and wonder how I'd get through the day. Then, I got involved in this huge community of shark conservation; it was something so different. I didn't know a soul in the shark conservation effort. It was a whole new place for me, and I found myself again. There was another version of me, buried down deep. By resetting myself and getting involved with something, I found my fury. I found myself. While this was going on, I was able to get out of my marriage with a lot of help. After that, I had a new clarity to my life."

Nova is still a work in progress, and Sue feels they are just getting started. They made over $38 million in revenue the year before our interview with only seventy-five employees.

A few years ago, Sue bought a small farm in Oregon where she met a wonderful man, and they are now engaged to be married. Sue's life experiences with her father's death, creating Nova from scratch, giving people stylish mobility, and helping save the sharks have enabled her to finally understand her own inner strength.

"The power is within me to make amazing things happen for the greater good. I have a purpose in this world. I was not put on this earth to be a bystander. I can't deny that. I am a force. Whether I like it or not, I am."

Paul Lehman

"You could be the most horrible human being in the world. But if you are a good producer and make a lot of money, people think you are a genius."

Paul Lehman lives in Salt Lake City, which he describes as almost an accident. He was born in New York City and raised on the Upper West Side, and for much of his life, he expected he would stay in Manhattan and work on Wall Street.

Paul is a first-generation American. His mother escaped France before World War II started. His father was not so lucky. He was born in Poland, captured as a Polish Jew at age twelve, and spent four years in a concentration camp in Auschwitz until he was rescued by American troops.

Paul's parents came to America in the 1950s. His father started his own brokerage firm on Wall Street and became well known. His mother was an architect who became the first female partner for I. M. Pei's firm.

"My mother was introverted and quiet," Paul says. "She was an extraordinary woman, but low-key about her success. She was one of only four women admitted to MIT her freshman year, but she never made a big deal out of that.

"My dad is the life of the party, extroverted, a great storyteller. But he was damaged by losing his whole family, being in Auschwitz.

I would call him a pretty bad father. Not that he meant any harm. He's very different. I couldn't relate it to me because he never had any childhood. He went from being a twelve-year-old to being in Auschwitz until he was sixteen. I think that was difficult.

"At an early age, I felt like if I was going to do anything in this world, I was going to have to do it myself. I've always had a strong independent streak. I didn't want to be reliant on anybody. My childhood could have been way worse, but it wasn't easy."

Paul always assumed he would end up with a career on Wall Street in finance like his father. He went to private high schools and then to Vassar. Between his junior and senior years, he worked on Wall Street on the floor of the American Stock Exchange. He was the only summer associate to get a full-time job offer.

Paul turned down the offer and knew he was passing up a good opportunity.

"I would have been so wealthy if I'd done that. I mean, this is like working on the floor of the New York Stock Exchange in the eighties, in the nineties. I had the fantasy home-run job offer. I don't think it's as lucrative now as it was then."

Paul declined the job for two reasons. The first was that his father got him the job, and he didn't want to be seen as someone's kid at work. The second reason was that, while he loved the adrenaline rush of working on Wall Street, he didn't like what he saw it did to people. He felt like if he had taken the job, he would have been a divorced coke addict by the time he was thirty-five.

LESSON LEARNED: Successful father figures can impose challenges rather than provide support.

Paul knew he wouldn't be happy if he took the job. He wanted to create his own life, to find his own way. On Wall Street, people's self-worth is tied to how much money they make and their net worth. "You could be the most horrible human being in the world. But if you are a good producer and make a lot of money, people think you are a genius."

On Wall Street, no matter how much money a person makes, it's never enough because there is always someone who makes more.

Paul took a position marketing mutual funds for the New York Life insurance company. He hated the job, sitting there and watching the clock every day because he couldn't wait to get off work. He lasted a year.

Paul became fascinated by consumer product marketing, and he observed what Ben & Jerry's had done to create a premium ice cream brand. He felt like the hot chocolate market was getting commoditized by mass-produced chocolate mixes sold in boxes. He went to the New York Public Library to research the cocoa market, and a friend designed his first hot chocolate box for free.

He started out working on his idea at night, while he still had his day job at New York Life. Soon he went into a small store at Ninety-Second Street and Madison Avenue to pitch his hot chocolate. They ordered two cases. When they called him three days later, he thought something was wrong. They said they had already sold their two cases and needed two more cases.

Paul quit his day job and raised money from his family and friends.

Paul claimed his new company was offering the "world's best hot chocolate," a claim eventually backed up by Julia Child drinking his hot chocolate on *Good Morning America*. His hot chocolate won the outstanding beverage award at the International Fancy Food and Confection Show three years in a row.

Paul ran the hot chocolate business for five years. He knew he had a great product—he was getting all sorts of press and awards and had 4,000 customers across the United States. The problem was most customers only bought two or three boxes per year. At three dollars per box, it just wasn't a great business.

Paul received a modest offer for the company from a company that sold salad dressing, a summer seasonal product, and wanted a winter seasonal product to diversify. He accepted the offer and made enough money to pay back all of his investors—except for his parents and two others—and to take a three-week scuba-diving vacation in the Caribbean.

Through this experience, Paul realized that business isn't binary— when you become an entrepreneur, you think you will either win big or lose big, but sometimes you just end up in purgatory.

Paul was twenty-eight years old with no significant obligations in life beyond himself. He was planning to apply to business school but had missed the application deadlines. He talked his way into a small private equity company owned by three guys with expertise in consumer packaging. They recently bought an automotive aftermarket company in Montana.

The guy who sold the automotive aftermarket company to the private equity firm was in a cult and had believed the end of the world was coming. When it didn't come as expected, he found himself drowning in debt. It wasn't the end of the world, but it was the end of his ownership of his company.

The firm asked Paul to move to Bozeman, Montana. Until that point, Paul had lived his whole life in New York City, and he was young and ready for a new adventure. He decided Montana would be an interesting place to spend six months.

Paul loved Montana and was intrigued by the automotive after-market business. The company made electronic parts to make motorcycles and cars go faster. It wasn't hot chocolate; it was branded consumer products, which Paul understood from his hot chocolate business, but the profits were much better.

> **LESSON LEARNED:** Geographic separation from familiarity can be essential to finding oneself.

In 1997, Paul left Montana and went to Harvard Business School. After that, he went to work for a large private equity firm in New York: Bear Stearns Merchant Banking Group. Paul wanted to learn how to buy and sell companies, and he spent four years doing exactly that. He loved the work but hated that he wasn't involved in day-to-day business operations.

Paul always wanted to run a business—to actually *make stuff* and *make a difference.* He was interested in the automotive aftermarket business after his experience in Montana, and he started looking to buy a company. It was a fragmented market of small, niche companies, and Paul finally found one in Ogden, Utah, while he was still working at the private equity firm.

The Utah part was problematic, because Paul had met his wife at Harvard, and they were living together in New York. She had a great job at Pfizer that she wasn't going to leave. Paul convinced his wife he could be in Utah only three out of four weeks, and then spend the fourth week—and every weekend—back in New York. The owners in Ogden weren't quite ready to sell the whole business to Paul, but he was ready to take control of his life and exit the private equity firm. He invested $500,000 for a minority stake in the company. If he increased the value of the firm and they sold it, he would get a good financial return.

Six months after Paul started in Ogden his wife became pregnant with their first child. He eventually convinced her to quit her job and move to Utah for a "few years."

Over the four years that Paul was involved in the automotive aftermarket business, revenues grew from $6 million to $30 million, and profits rose from $1.5 million to $8 million. As Paul puts it, "to be successful in any business, you need three things: luck, skill, and timing. If you only have one of them, you're never going to make it. If you have two of them and you work really hard, you'll do okay. When you have all three, you're going to think you're a genius. I had all three in that deal."

They sold the business in 2006, before the 2008 market crash, for $62 million. Paul and his wife made enough money to stay in Utah for a while to figure out their next steps. By then, they had three kids.

LESSON LEARNED: Seekers are always looking for the next chance to learn.

Paul and his wife loved being outdoors and enjoyed the natural beauty of Utah. A few months after they sold the business, they invested in a bike business in Ogden. The bike business was consuming cash, and their efforts to hire a CEO were unsuccessful. Everything went wrong. Paul and his wife wanted to move to Salt Lake City or Park City, where the schools were better than Ogden, but the bike business required so much cash they had to decide between saving their investment or moving.

Paul's wife agreed to run the bike business, and it was tough going. It was a global business competing with bikes made cheaply in China or Vietnam. At one point, Paul and his wife were down to around $150,000 in cash and had to sell their pickup truck to pay tuition money for their kid's private education. After nine years they finally sold the business.

It's not as if every investment Paul and his wife made worked out. Paul made some real estate investments with some of the cash from the sale. He loves Montana, and he bought a one-acre ski lot in Big Sky. He thought it could be a ski retreat for his family after they moved back to Chicago to be closer to his wife's family in Green Bay. However, Paul couldn't have timed the Big Sky real estate deal worse. He bought the property for a little over $1 million, but when the bike business started chewing up all their liquidity, he had to sell it for about $350K to raise cash.

Paul doesn't remember many conversations with his wife about their liquidity problems. Their kids were young back then, and they figured that if they needed to, they could just start over. What he does remember as stressful was all the overseas travel that his wife needed to do to meet with suppliers for the bike business.

> **LESSON LEARNED:** Finding oneself often requires going against expectations.

In 2011, Paul took the proceeds from the Montana real estate sale and invested it in another automotive aftermarket company in Austin, Texas. It turned out to be a great business. He sold his stake four years later at a profit of around $5 million, and that solved their liquidity problems. It was the only business Paul's invested in where he feels he sold too early.

Paul has always had a sense of adventure, and he wanted to create his own life. Early on he seemed headed for a New York City–based Wall Street career, but that all changed when he fell in love with the Mountain West.

"Listen, I have friends that can't move north of Fourteenth Street in Manhattan. Yes, it was unusual. I'm not sure I would have done it, had I not had the opportunity to go to Montana in the nineties. I had nothing in New York. I mean, it just seemed like fun for a little while, an adventure. I ended up loving it out here. But yes, I'm wired differently than most people that way."

Paul is notably low-key about taking risk, but he admits his view is changing in his mid-fifties. When he was younger, it was easier for him to risk everything:

"When we first moved to Utah, and I left Bear Stearns Merchant Banking group, my wife left her job and we put it all in the business out here. We had one six-month-old kid and I didn't see much downside. I mean, there was definitely risk because I don't think I would've been able to get a job at another private equity firm because once you leave that, it's tough to get back in. But it didn't seem like we were losing that much. We were both pretty young. We're both Harvard MBAs and my wife is unbelievably employable. It didn't seem that bad."

Today, Paul and his wife are invested in two businesses: a small company making parts to help motorcycles go faster, and a coffee-maker business that lets people make premium coffees at home. Both investments are making progress, but could go either way. Paul has learned that you need to get to $10 million or more in revenue before you can think about paying yourself a salary or cashing out.

But, by his own admission, Paul has a different "floor" on risk-taking now that his kids are getting older.

> **LESSON LEARNED:** Hindsight and age elevate the risk floor that risk-takers tolerate.

Paul is living the life he has chosen, not the one that seemed predestined for him in New York. He cares about adventure, about his family, and about finding his own path. He has no regrets about the huge and unconventional risks he's taken.

If we can learn anything from the stories of Jim Fallon, Peter Denning, Sue Chen, and Paul Lehman it is that finding yourself inevitably involves some pain and searching—and that the events of your life are not actually within your control, no matter how much you wish they were.

Jim's traditional career path of MBA to strategy consulting firm to entrepreneurship was dramatically altered by his cancer diagnosis and recovery. Sue had to overcome the tragic death of her father and an abusive marriage to really find her path; and it was only when she became a spokesperson for shark conservation that she found her voice. Peter struggled for years, despite his enormous business talent, to find himself in the shadow of a dominant father. He had to quit his job, move halfway across the world, and create an entirely new adventure to choose his own life path in the face of pressure from his parents. And Paul had to escape the confines of the New York City financial world to find his life's calling.

Finding yourself is never easy, but it seems to be a necessary step on the path to a fulfilling life. For those who do find themselves, taking a risk is often the price.

In the end, risk-takers who focus on finding themselves learn they must change in response to the events of their lives: the accomplishments *and* the tragedies. Their stories are stories of courage and perseverance—the courage to find yourself and learn how you can best serve those around you.

CHAPTER NINE

Givers

Many risk-takers follow Abraham Maslow's hierarchy of needs as they formulate the trajectory of their lives. Once they take care of material needs for themselves and those they are close to, they focus more on love and belonging, self-esteem, and self-actualization.

We tend to think of risks as risking money and job opportunities. But we found that belonging, self-esteem, and the very concept of self, all require significant courage—and just as many disruptive leaps.

Sojourner Truth was a Giver who took risks throughout her life to establish freedom and individual rights. Isabella Baumfree was born a slave in rural New York in 1797. She was sold three times before age thirteen, and finally escaped at age twenty-nine.

Soon after, she learned her son Peter was sold as a slave in New York and taken to Alabama. This was a violation of the recently passed New York State Emancipation Act. Isabella fought for legal assistance and won Peter's return to New York, becoming the first black woman to win such a case against a white man.

Isabella and Peter moved to New York City, and she found her voice. Although she didn't know how to read or write, she started by giving inspiring testimony in a black Methodist congregation.

With her newfound calling, Isabella freed herself with a new name, Sojourner Truth. She first made her mark as an itinerant preacher and evangelist, becoming famous during a speaker tour with a well-known radical member of the British Parliament, George Thompson.

After the beginning of the Civil War, she re-fashioned herself into an abolitionist and recruited many blacks to serve in the Union Army. Later in life, she became an antislavery feminist. Improbably, Sojourner Truth became one of the most well-known black women of the nineteenth century, meeting with the abolitionist author Harriet Beecher Stowe, Presidents Lincoln and Grant, and the women's suffrage advocate Susan B. Anthony.

Sojourner was exceptionally good at networking, as many Givers are. One of her biographers wrote, "in each of the three great chapters of Sojourner Truth's life—slavery, evangelism, and antislavery feminism—she built networks of human contact. These networks sustained her materially and spiritually, steadily broadening her horizons."[16]

In the end, many risk-takers focus on "giving back." It is often their own unique way to express gratitude for the life they have been given, and for paying back those who have given to them.

James Ellis

"I was hoping like hell a parachute would open
before I went splat on the canyon floor."

Jim Ellis was born in Tacoma, Washington, in 1947. Jim's father was
a commercial banker who moved frequently for his career—first
from Washington to California, then to New Mexico when Jim
was in the eighth grade. Jim went to high school in Albuquerque
and then to the University of New Mexico on a golf scholarship.

What Jim really wanted to be was a professional golfer. His dad
taught him how to play when he was seven, and that started an
addiction that, sixty-five years later, he still has not shaken. He was
a good enough golfer to make his college team at New Mexico, but
not quite good enough to make it as a pro.

When Jim graduated from New Mexico, he wanted to take a shot
at making it on the golf tour, but his dad convinced him to apply
to business school as a fallback option. He decided to apply to the
four best business schools in the country, hoping he would not get
admitted so that he could just play golf. This seemed like a logical
plan, given that he was only an average student at New Mexico,
which was no more than an average school itself. He needed a
faculty recommendation to even apply to business school, and this
was a dilemma since he hadn't gone to class that much. Indeed, in
four years he had never even been in a professor's office.

When he finally walked into the office to request a letter of recommendation, the professor didn't recognize him as someone who
had been in his class. After some back and forth, the professor
asked him to stay for a chat so that he could get to know him a
bit. Forty-five minutes into the conversation, the professor asked
Jim what business school he wanted to get into. Knowing he had

no chance to get into Harvard, which was good since he really just wanted to play golf, Jim told the professor that he wanted to go to Harvard.

Unfortunately, the professor happened to know the dean of admissions at Harvard Business School. He picked up the phone, dialed the dean, and said, "I've got a guy here that I want to recommend for your incoming class. He's one of my students. He's doing fine in my class. I just have a sneaky feeling someday this guy's going to do okay in life. And I think you ought to take him."

The next thing Jim knew, he was admitted to Harvard Business School, with a 2.87 grade point average from the University of New Mexico. He was twenty-one years old and pretty intimidated by Harvard when he got there. After a few weeks, though, he began to feel like he could hold his own. He says, "Harvard Business School was a tough place to be, but a great place to be from. I just truly enjoyed the experience. I learned an awful lot."

After Harvard, Jim came back to the West Coast, mostly because the weather was cold in Boston, and he wanted to play golf again. He got a job in Los Angeles with Broadway Department Stores, which had forty-plus retail department stores. He soon found out that it was more of a seven-days-a-week than a five-days-a-week position. He ended up spending nine and a half years there, mostly as a buyer. Meanwhile, his golf game suffered terribly.

By 1983, Jim was thirty-six and working for a small apparel distribution company in San Diego. He was planning to buy the company from its founder, who was a golfing buddy of his dad. It was a small business with about $5 million in revenue. They had thirty people on the road selling apparel to golf shops and another twenty who were selling apparel to the military.

Jim ended up buying the business. Soon after doing so, he came across a discount chain starting up down the street. They were looking for apparel because no one would sell to them. Luckily for Jim, they were the first Price Club—which later became Costco. From that single customer, Jim's business went from $5 million to $80 million in annual revenue very quickly.

Jim ended up selling the business back to the founder after a few years. The founder had never really left the business and was just too difficult to work with. He had three sets of books and wasn't a nice guy. Jim got burned on the deal financially, or at least didn't make what he should have for growing the business so quickly. But he learned a lot about negotiation and made sure that he didn't make the same mistakes again.

> **LESSON LEARNED:** Walking through the door of risk opens up opportunity one way or another.

Jim was in the middle of fighting with the founder over money when he went on a blind date. He was thirty-eight years old and had been living the single guy life since college. The woman lived in Chicago, but she and Jim got along well. Two months later, he asked her to go skiing with him for a week in Colorado. During that week, only their second time together, he asked her to marry him. The woman had four children.

In the space of a few weeks, Jim went from owning a company to being unemployed—and from being a single, unattached guy to being engaged to a woman with four kids, who lived thousands of miles away. Even looking back now on a lifetime of risk, Jim says this was the biggest risk he ever took. But he just knew intuitively that it was going to work.

We asked him what was going through his mind:

"Well, first of all, because I was thirty-eight and had been a pretty active bachelor, I knew good from bad and I knew great from good. So, when you get to that point in your life, you can decide pretty quickly whether this person is what you're looking for or not. I could tell just by the way she talked about her kids. And I had never been married, never been engaged, never lived with anyone. It was one of those things. When it's right, it's right."

When he first met Gail's four kids, they were thirteen, nine, seven, and five years old. And that was after he and Gail were engaged. The oldest, a boy, wanted golf clubs for his eighth-grade graduation; and if there was anything Jim could help a teenage boy with, it was buying golf clubs. They remain an incredibly close family to this day, thirty-four years later.

> **LESSON LEARNED:** Personal risks can be the invisible backbone allowing professional risk.

Jim looked for a new job as they planned the wedding. He was thinking it needed to be in Chicago, but his wife-to-be told him that she and the kids would move to wherever he found work.

He landed a job as president of American Porsche Design in Los Angeles, working for the Austrian-based Porsche family. American Porsche Design sold everything with the Porsche name on it except for the cars themselves—leather goods, sunglasses, watches, etc. The job went well and lasted six years. He reported directly into the Porsche family and attended board meetings in Salzburg, Austria, four times a year. The job ended when the exchange rate became unfavorable to selling cars in the United States, and the family needed to cut costs. They offered Jim the role of CEO for the whole company, but it was based in Austria, and he wouldn't move his family there.

Instead, Jim stayed in Los Angeles and started buying and selling companies with a couple of partners. It was during a buyout boom when you could buy small companies for not much money down, and then take out the rest of the money in debt. Over the next six years, Jim and his partners bought and sold nine companies—and they did well financially.

By then, Jim had joined the YPO group. At one of the forum meetings, the woman running the group asked Jim, "What are you going to do with the next twenty-five years of your life?" The forum group gave him thirty days to come back with a presentation. Jim gave it a great deal of thought, and when he came back, he told the group that he wanted to spend the next twenty-five years helping others avoid some of the speed bumps in life that he had learned about the hard way. His group told him, "Great, now go figure out how to do that." Jim tried to protest that he had a wife and five kids (they had since added one to the family). But the forum group wasn't buying any excuses.

About a week after the forum group meeting, a friend requested a meeting with Jim. Over breakfast, the guy told him that the University of Southern California Business School was looking for a marketing professor to teach a class. Jim agreed to go on the interview. Three days before his fiftieth birthday, he started work as a marketing professor. He had no idea how he was going to support his family, but he knew it was the right move, the right risk to take.

"It was my midlife crisis. I had gone from being an entrepreneur to teaching a marketing class full-time. And that was my transition. It was a real, seminal change."

Jim was still running a company in Pasadena when he started teaching three marketing classes. He found that he could teach the three classes and still have time left over for running a business. But the more he taught, the more he loved the classroom. Within six months, he exited his ownership position in all three companies he was involved with. His wife was totally supportive of this major career change and believed they would find a way to make it work.

Jim recalls, "The way I looked at this was, if you remember Wile E. Coyote and the Road Runner, the Road Runner would run off the cliff and the Coyote would chase him. But the Road Runner can fly back onto the cliff and the Coyote would fall to the canyon floor. Well, I was living like the Coyote, hoping like hell a parachute would open before I went splat on the canyon floor. I had taken a risk to go from doing very, very well financially to not doing so well. I mean, my starting salary as a full-time marketing professor was $65,000 a year. That wasn't going to pay the bills for a wife and five kids. So, I would augment it with consulting and speaking and all kinds of stuff, and it turned out to be pretty lucrative."

Jim's dive off the cliff worked. What started out as a teaching assignment for a few classes and a modest salary turned into becoming Dean of the USC Business School for the last twelve years (we talked to Jim four days after he went on sabbatical after twelve years of running the business school). It's now been twenty-two years since Jim swapped his corporate career for academia.

"Basically, I just taught for the first couple of years. Then they put me in charge of the family business program. So, I built a family business program for USC, but I was still a full-time professor. And then about six years into the mission, they asked, 'Would you be the dean of the undergraduate program?' And I said, 'Only if I get to keep teaching.' And they said, 'Yeah, you can teach, but we want you to be the dean of the undergrad program.' So, I did that for a little while.

"At some point I stopped teaching full-time, taught one class, which I have continued to do until now, and was in charge of external relations for the business school. Then I became the vice provost of the university, in charge of all the global aspects of the school. I did that for a couple of years, building relationships with Chinese and European universities, corporations, and governments. Everybody was talking about globalization. We achieved that. In April of 2007, I was asked by the provost of the university to be the dean of the business school."

Jim's time at USC has been all about giving back. The difference between Jim and other people is that many people wait until they are in their sixties to think about giving back. Jim thought about it differently.

"A lot of people say, 'When I retire, I want to give back.' My give-back was to get involved in the academic world, even though I didn't think about it that way. It's been my give-back to society, trying to help build this next generation of kids. How do I prepare these kids for the life they're going to lead?"

Looking back, Jim has no regrets. He realizes he could have made more money had he stayed in the corporate world, but he understands that through his work at USC he made major contributions to business school education and, along the way, many students' lives. He also took a massive risk in his marriage to a woman with four kids, but it ended up working spectacularly well. He understands that he took another risk going into teaching without knowing how he was going to support his growing family, but that worked out well too.

There's an equanimity that emanates from Jim that can only be acquired through life experience. During his interview with Alan, Southern California experienced a major earthquake. When it hits, Jim explains very calmly that an earthquake is happening, and he needs to take a break for a minute or two.

As Jim puts it simply, "I have a pretty cool thing going."

Gene Gobolys

"It's no mystery to me that I see risk differently than a lot of folks do. To me, that was my competitive advantage."

Gene Gobolys grew up in Toledo, Ohio, in a large Catholic family, the sixth of seven children. He now lives in Boston with his wife Jacqueline, known as Jacque, who is from Buenos Aires, Argentina. Gene and Jacque have five children, three of whom are adopted and two by birth.

Several things happened to Gene during his childhood that shaped his life.

The first is that his parents lived with unfulfilled career and life ambitions. Gene's father wanted to be an airline pilot. He never went to college. He served in World War II and was in pilot training, but the military had too many pilots and too few turret gunners, so he was moved to being a turret gunner when he was only a couple of hours away from getting a pilot's license. He spent most of his career as a salesman.

Gene's mom was more intellectually inclined, and she went to Stanford. After Stanford, she was going to be stationed in Hawaii, but she came from a strict and traditional Italian family; her father demanded she return to Ohio, where she ended up working as a physical therapist and raising a large family.

Gene picked up early on his mom's intellectualism and grew up curious about the world. He understood that he didn't want to let his own dreams for life be unfulfilled, as he sensed a certain sadness in both parents.

"My mother clearly had bigger expectations for me than she did for any of my siblings," he says. "I'm not entirely sure why that was. I think my brother might've just got washed in the early cabal of a bunch of kids. She had high expectations of me from the get-go. For her, the highest expectation was that I would be the first American pope."

Gene learned early on that he wanted to take risks with his life, in part because he didn't see either his parents or his siblings doing so.

"The riskiest thing I could see ahead of me as a little boy was following my siblings' footsteps. It felt like there was this assembly-line experience ahead of me, and that I would go through these predictable schools and then to whatever state school in Ohio and then get a job. I was watching my siblings go and get their first jobs and marching through the mechanics of it. There didn't seem to be any joy in any of it. I never saw anybody taking wild chances, and that turned out to be a bad thing. I liked risk from early on."

LESSON LEARNED: Some risk-takers have early life experiences imprinting the value of risk.

Another event in Gene's childhood had a profound effect on his life, and even shaped his career direction. His uncle, who owned his own business and had ten children, was a well-known industrialist but was always fighting to keep his company afloat. Gene's father was spending a ton of time with this uncle—Gene's mom's brother—as he tried to save his company.

When Gene was thirteen, his uncle had a breakdown. He just couldn't deal with the business pressure and the loss of stature with having a struggling company. One day his grandmother called, looking for his mom. Gene took the call. Gene's uncle had committed suicide.

Gene saw first-hand the horrendous effect this tragedy had on everyone. His father lived the rest of his life with the feeling that he should have done more to help, but he had seven kids and financial pressures of his own. Gene spent a great deal of time with one of his cousins whose father had just killed himself. As a result of this, he would later shape his career around helping business owners who are in trouble. "That was hugely impactful," he says today. "I'm still impacted by trying to not have regrets, to have seen something and not taking enough action."

Gene quickly figured out that the only way to get money was to make some himself. When he was fourteen, he asked a neighbor if he could mow her lawn and she said, "No, I don't need you to mow my lawn, but I would like you to paint some houses for me."

It turned out Gene's neighbor was also a slumlord: she owned thirty houses in some rough neighborhoods of Toledo. She had a nephew named Michael who lived in inner-city Baltimore. She asked Gene to partner with Michael to paint the houses she rented out. Gene did this for the next three summers.

Painting houses in the inner city was another formative experience for Gene, a white kid, who experienced considerable hostility while he worked in the mainly black neighborhoods. But Gene and Michael became fast friends, made lots of money, and had a good time working together. Michael, who was black, protected Gene in threatening situations. Gene began to see the world from a more tolerant perspective than he was used to.

After high school, Gene went off to study economics at Ohio State. He nearly flunked out his sophomore year from partying too much. But then he made a friend who was more serious about school, and they moved into an apartment together for their junior and senior years.

After graduation, Gene got a job with a minority business development center in downtown Columbus and started writing business plans for minority entrepreneurs. When Gene was twenty-three years old, he decided to move to Portland, Maine. His boss asked him what he was going to do in Portland. Gene said, "I have no idea." His boss told him that he would regret the decision forever.

"I moved to Maine. Not knowing a soul, I slept on a fishing boat the first night, then snuck into the YMCA. I got myself a shower and then found a job as a bartender. That was on March 3, 1987. I remember that because it's my mom's birthday. My parents could not figure out why in the hell I was going to a place where I knew no one. But I had been to Portland the year before in the summertime, and it was beautiful and I was really drawn to how nature and the community were interwoven. People had a much better sense for the outdoors and for being healthy than back in Ohio.

"I got a room for $55 a night; I had gone out there with $300 in my pocket. By the time I was down to $100, I didn't have enough money to go eat and pay for gas to get back home, so I had to make it work."

"I needed to immediately generate positive cash flow. I started getting tips in my bartender job. I got to know a lot of people and really liked the town. I thought I'd be a real estate developer, which is hard to do on no money. But I took a course up there studying real estate and got to know a few local real estate developers. I realized I should be looking for gigs where there were more people. In November of that year, I moved down to Boston and took a job at Harvard. I couldn't believe that I could get a job at this place that seemed so far beyond my reach."

The job at Harvard was managing research grants. The work was boring, but Gene loved the Harvard environment. He went to see incredible speakers on the campus every day; he even played basketball at lunch with Bill Walton. He took courses at Harvard's extension program just to learn, with no real degree in mind.

Gene grew interested in city planning. Through a contact at Harvard, he began working in Boston to revive Kendall Square, which was then a heavy industrial area. He found the city planning work intriguing, but was frustrated that plans took years to implement.

Next, Gene went to work for the Massachusetts state government in economic development. There was an old Proctor & Gamble soap plant that the company wanted to shut down. Gene helped secure state money to transition the plant into a biodiesel company that turned trash into energy, since the plant had all the infrastructure for handling chemicals. Ultimately, the effort didn't work because the ex-P&G guys running the plant didn't understand the biodiesel market. From this experience Gene became hooked on the clean energy market. It was right after the Gulf War, and Gene felt that clean energy was going to be an important market to secure US energy independence from the Persian Gulf.

When Gene left state government, he was admitted to the Kennedy School of Government at Harvard. By that time, his focus had shifted from economic development to entrepreneurship. He was getting tired of not having money in his pocket. Then in 1998, Gene decided it was time to jump off the cliff and start his own trash-to-biodiesel energy company. He called the company World Energy, which, grandiose name aside, was a one-man operation founded on credit card debt.

One month into the new business he had a new problem: his girlfriend, Jacque, was pregnant. Suddenly, his world looked very different. Gene was going to give up on World Energy, but Jacque would not have it.

"She was the real risk-taker, not me. She told me that she would be offended if I quit because of our situation, and that she was along for the ride no matter what. If she needed to support me, then she would do whatever was needed."

> **LESSON LEARNED:** Spousal support
> is key to many risk-takers' success.

With no safety net, Gene kept going, knocking on doors and finding contracts for World Energy. An early turning point was when he met with the CEO of Gulf Oil, based in Boston, and convinced the company to guarantee his credit line in exchange for a small equity stake in the business.

Gene leveraged everything he could to borrow money and get the business off the ground. He began buying small, troubled manufacturing companies to secure more plant capacity for World Energy. It took him until 2008, twelve years after he founded the business, to begin generating a couple of million dollars a year in profits.

Gene was on a mission to make the business work. He believed in the risk, giving him confidence to handle the stress.

"I was never nervous. There was one point where I bought our first house, and I didn't have the money to make the payments. It was getting uncomfortable. There were times I was a pretty bad credit risk. But no, I wasn't ever particularly nervous about it. As crazy as it sounds, I do keep track of absolutely every penny. I'm really detailed in terms of exactly where the money is coming in from and where it's going out to, which at least gave me a sense of control."

Gene and Jacque were married on Easter in 1999, a few years after their first child was born. He and Jacque are both from large Catholic families. They had their second child shortly after they married, but they had difficulty conceiving a third child and started going down the path to adopt. Around this time, their kids started playing with two brothers a few years older than them, who were from a multifamily home down the street. Jacque met the kids' mother at school, a young, single mother who wasn't able to raise the kids on her own.

Soon after that, the younger brother, who was then in third grade, came over to their house and never left. The older brother went back and forth between houses for a while before moving in. Gene and his wife eventually adopted the two brothers with their mother's consent, and they raised them as part of the family.

"It was clear from early on that they needed more structure and more warmth and more love and more guidance and more food and more shelter and more of everything. The ironic thing was we were in the middle of an adoption process. We were looking halfway around the world to adopt a kid from disadvantaged circumstances in Guatemala. Are we going to overlook the ones that are right in front of us? I think our hearts and minds were open. It was never our intention to add these two kids to our family. It just happened."

The adopted boys' mother was wholly supportive of this move. She was from Haiti, and the Haitian tradition is that communities raise children, not just the parents.

LESSON LEARNED: The risk-taker mindset is applicable to professional *and* personal risks.

Gene feels his marriage and growing his family was one of the biggest risks he ever took, but he is delighted with how it has turned out. He took significant risks in his business, often growing through debt-financed acquisition. But he remains matter-of-fact as he explains these decisions, so matter-of-fact that it's easy to miss the significance of them. He now has three hundred employees and a growing company.

Gene feels that, in a cyclical business, his orientation toward risk and willingness to take unusual risks is a competitive advantage.

"It's no mystery to me that I see risk differently than a lot of folks do. To me, that was my competitive advantage. That's the core competency. If you're going to be in one of these crazy businesses, why wait around until it's doing great to make your next move? When it's doing great, everybody else in the business is doing great. You've got to buy other businesses during the down cycle."

Gene is driven by giving back, by making the world a better place. He's been able to do so by having a mission-driven business, where he's helped many of his managers find professional success—but also through his unique family structure.

Ivo Nelson

"Millions of dollars don't mean jack-shit when you're lonely."

Ivo Nelson grew up in Waco, Texas. His father was a pharmaceutical rep and his mom was a teacher. After high school, he worked as a ranch hand in the Texas Hill Country. He spent a few years being what he calls "footloose and fancy free," traveling in the West and doing construction work in San Francisco. Then he came back to Waco and got a business degree at Baylor University.

Ivo was always wired for business but never thought too much about money. "I really had no desire for a fancy lifestyle," he says. "Coming out of high school, I was doing mundane construction work. I was more inclined toward the nonprofit, give-back type of job. I was even going to pursue a degree in recreational therapy. That was originally what I wanted to do.

"Somewhere along the line, I shifted to business. The business side of it was always in my blood, even when I was a little boy. I was a kid who would go trick or treating and save all my candy. I'd save it so long it would go bad. I mowed lawns, delivered papers, and had the snow cone machine out in the front yard, selling snow cones. I was an ice cream man for two years in high school. The idea of working hard and being a businessperson was just how I was wired."

While money wasn't important to Ivo, succeeding was. After Baylor, he went to work for EDS, the information technology company founded by Ross Perot. He spent seven years there, until Perot was ousted when General Motors bought the business. Perot started up Perot Systems, and Ivo went to work for him and ended up running the healthcare business for the next four years.

"I eventually left Perot because I'd married a woman who was the chief financial officer at Texas Children's Hospital. I was living in Dallas. She was planning on moving to Dallas. I was lying in bed one night and thought, *Why am I asking her to move? She's got this job at this place that people love, and she has been a big part of making it successful.* I'm a flexible guy, so I just said, 'Let me see if I can get something figured out in Houston.'

"I ran into a guy who had written a business plan and sold the idea to Rod Canion, founder of Compaq Computers. He had left Compaq the year prior, and so I made the decision to join up with them and helped them start that company. After the first year, I was running the company."

The company that Ivo joined was a consulting and IT outsourcing business. The firm would start out doing process consulting work with the goal of taking over the IT department. The only vertical market where the business really got off the ground was healthcare, which Ivo ran, so he ended up running the whole firm after the other vertical market efforts failed.

Ivo grew the company for the next thirteen years. They expanded their geographic focus from Texas to the West Coast, and then eventually to England, Europe, and the Middle East. The business was doing well enough that some board members wanted to sell out, but Ivo convinced them to wait longer. He wasn't the kind of CEO who was going to get pushed around by his board, and he was confident he could continue to increase the value of the company.

Ivo eventually sold the business in 2005 to IBM and made lots of money, but, ironically, he remembers 2005 as the worst year of his life.

"I won the Ernst & Young Entrepreneur of the Year award that year. I won several other awards in healthcare, and I was at what you would think to be the absolute peak of success. And yet, on the other hand, personally, being a loser. I got divorced.

"There's a very clear memory I have of working for IBM and doing a huge amount of global travel, then coming home and walking into a house that I bought just up the street from my ex-wife, because we still had a daughter. I wanted her to be golf cart–driving distance between the two houses. Walking into this house with a whole bunch of brand spanking new furniture, fresh paint, brand new carpet. It had that new, crisp feel to it, a bunch of crap put up on shelves that I had a decorator to put up there that meant nothing to me. I remember standing in the middle of the living room, falling down on my knees, and starting to cry. I realized that while I had everything I could have ever dreamed of having, I had lost everything that was important to me: my family."

KEY CONCEPT—INNER FULFILLMENT
RISK: Those who have everything, materially, still may experience emptiness. Their next risks are about inner fulfillment.

"Right then, I made a commitment to win my wife back. There's a whole romantic story around that process. But at the end of the day, I did. We were divorced in March. We were remarried in December and, by the way, the IRS doesn't recognize a divorce if it happens inside a tax year. This was a life lesson. I mean, you can have everything, you can lose everything. Millions of dollars don't mean jack-shit when you're sad and lonely."

Ivo and his wife had grown apart because they were so busy with their careers. "It was like a lot of divorces. It starts off with anger and resentment, and it just starts eating at you. And then next thing you know, it blows up." It wasn't easy for him to win her back, since she had started emotionally disconnecting from the relationship. He began by sitting down with her and telling her he wanted to get back together. She wasn't ready to commit to that, but on the other hand she didn't say no. He sent her a romantic greeting card every single day. Tentatively, they started dating again. Eventually, he asked her to remarry him.

Looking back, Ivo says, "In many ways, the divorce was by far the best thing that ever happened to us, because it forced both of us into the zones where we could cool our jets; relax a bit, with that tension all gone away; realize that the anger and the things we thought were important really weren't. They were little things. And we missed each other."

In 2005, Ivo made, for the first time, a lot of money. More money than he ever thought he would have in his life. Yet, he almost lost his family. It didn't help that he sold the healthcare consulting company, by then called Healthlink, to IBM. As good as the sale price was, Ivo was a fish out of water at IBM. They had him traveling all over the world, but he no longer had any authority and had no idea how to work across the IBM organization.

Ivo left IBM and decided to start another business. From ground zero at his kitchen table. He didn't need the money; it was just in his blood to keep working.

This time, instead of becoming CEO, Ivo provided most of the funding and served as board chair. That company, Encore, was also a healthcare tech consulting company. The business was another huge success, growing from $4 million to $20 million to $40 million to $65 million in annual revenue. Then Ivo and the board decided to sell it.

Alan met Ivo at an industry trade show while he was still running Healthlink. They both have big personalities and love to talk about business and risk, especially how people in business process and deal with risk.

Ivo's views on risk-taking have changed as he's gotten older.

"The sixty-three-year-old Ivo probably would not have made the same decisions that the thirty-two-year-old Ivo made, because I know enough now to understand that those were the really risky decisions. But the beauty of it is that that's why entrepreneurs succeed. It's because they do things without having any comprehension of the risk. They just do it anyway. They do things they shouldn't do and they win. I can look back at a lot of things I've done that I wouldn't do again, but somehow, it worked. I think there's a component of luck, but there's also a component of just working hard, grinding it out.

"Most people have no idea how hard it is. That's one answer. Knowing what I know today, I probably would change decisions. But on the other hand, if I were to change any of those decisions, I wouldn't be sitting where I am right now and I couldn't be in a better position. I mean, I absolutely would not want to change anything because my life is so perfect right now. The one area

I'd have second thoughts on is spending more time with my kids. That's the one thing I wish I had done more."

> **LESSON LEARNED:** This is Livewith Five
> in action—risk tastes different with age.

Ivo conceptualized his business career as unfolding in three stages: leading a company to success with money from external investors, leading a company to success with his own money, and finally having enough money to become an active angel investor. All three stages are complete. But the journey has had many twists and turns.

Having created two enormous, successful companies, Ivo now wants to give back through helping businesses create healthier and more meaningful work cultures. He has written a book called *The Ten Principles of a Love-Based Culture: How Authentic Business Leaders Trust Their Employees to Do the Right Thing.* "It's not about romantic love," Ivo says. "It's about building a love-based culture that makes money and has a positive impact on the world. One of the lessons I learned from the IBM experience is that IBM and many other companies use fear. Everything is designed around creating a fear-based culture. Even down to how compensation programs work, how policies and procedures are set up. Nobody trusts anybody in the organization to make decisions, so they have to have layers and layers of bureaucracy. Those tenets, ultimately, are not as good a way to run a business. With *a love-based culture,* you've got happier people. You have fewer divorces. You've got care and love in the workplace. It's just a better business. You make more money. Investors are happier."

Kirk Craig

"Everybody has a plan until they get punched in the face."

Kirk Craig has found meaning and given back in a different way than any of the risk-takers we have highlighted so far. He grew up in Memorial, Texas, a wealthy suburb of Houston where his parents live to this day. His father ran a successful family dry cleaning business until he and Kirk's uncle sold it.

Kirk has consciously chosen the life that he has. Kirk grew up in the Baptist church, and his faith had a huge impact on his life direction. He went to a private Christian school. After sixth grade, his class went on a church mission to Mexico, and his experience there was formative to his development.

"We drove from Houston in those twelve- and fifteen-passenger vans, probably a hundred of us, sixty teenagers, forty adults. We went and did services there. I had this clear impression while I was there seeing Mexican boys running around and playing in poverty that there was nothing I had done to get to where I was. The family I'd been born into, the privileges I knew I had—I hadn't earned any of that. I could've just as easily been born in Reynosa, Mexico, and had a different life. And the question that I walked away with from there was, *Why?* What should I be doing in light of that? Why should I have what I have, and what should I do because of that? I continued to do those trips all throughout my schooling."

Kirk went to college at the University of Virginia and majored in economics, graduating in 2000. After college, he had multiple opportunities including going to work in Charlotte in commercial banking or returning to Houston to work with his father in the family business.

"I hit this fork in the road. The Christmas right before graduation, I got an offer to work for First Union in Charlotte to go through a two-year training program in their commercial banking division, and then come out and be a banker. A minister I knew was going to a rural village in eastern Bolivia where I had been, at a mission in San Ignacio de Velasco. He said, 'Why don't you come with me?'

"I remember that Christmas break, I went to the Arboretum, a nature preserve in Houston, to think about it. I prayed and spent the whole day there trying to figure it out. Honestly, I was asking God, *What am I supposed to do? I'll do whatever you want me to do. What do you want me to do here?* I did not get a parting of the clouds, writing in the sky, some sign, or Bible verse that said, *Go do this.* But I had this sense of God putting it back on me like, *Well, what do you want to do? My presence is going to be with you wherever you are. So, you pick.'*

"I wanted to be a part of this mission down in Bolivia and to try to help the youth there. So, I told First Union, 'Nope,' and declined their offer. I told this minister, 'Yes, I'm coming,' and I started preparing for that. Once I graduated and even before, I started making plans, getting training, raising funds to be able to do this."

> **LESSON LEARNED:** Seeing is believing—
> money does not guarantee a meaningful life.

Kirk was confident that the decision to go to Bolivia was going to work out. From his privileged upbringing, he had gotten to know plenty of unhappy millionaires, so he knew that money wasn't going to guarantee happiness. He was also cognizant, even at a young age, that his decision to go to Bolivia would lead him down a track away from the business world, and that this probably meant he would have less money as he raised his family.

What Kirk didn't understand when he left for Bolivia was exactly how hard the experience itself would be.

"I go to Bolivia. And I think I'm a good public speaker. I can speak Spanish. I've got this economics degree. I've been leading this student ministry for four years. I'd had a summer there. I'd built relationships. I'm going to do well at this. And little by little, all of that confidence was eroded by experiences of failure. Like trying to develop local leadership and having them completely abandon responsibilities, whether it was religious or family or work responsibilities; trying to start programs with local youth that failed; trying some economic development projects where guys couldn't stay sober to complete the training. It was a real humbling season for me.

"Yet it was exciting, and I got to try a lot of different things in the organization. They let me try some out-of-the-box projects like the carpentry training program for young men. I traded the computer that I came down with to a local carpenter in exchange for him to train young men in carpentry. Three of the four washed out of the class. We had a bakery helping single moms sell fresh bread. They went through the seed money multiple times; they just ate it or spent it. We had a lot of trial and error during that time."

Kirk had met his wife Amanda when he was four, and pursued her through high school and college. They stayed in touch and were good friends, but she wasn't willing to date him—she felt he was too intense and serious. After three months in Bolivia, he asked her to join him on the mission. She had a master's degree in social work and nonprofit experience working in the inner city of Houston.

She agreed to join him in Bolivia, and their relationship blossomed.

Before they got married, Amanda gave Kirk a book called *Real Hope in Chicago*, written by a community activist named Wayne L. Gordon. It was the story of how Wayne developed a Christian community development in the Lawndale neighborhood of Chicago. The book shaped Kirk's vision of what he wanted to do with his life. He saw the importance of using his faith to help low-income communities build practical skills.

LESSON LEARNED: All-consuming mission increases personal risk tolerance.

Kirk and Amanda married in February 2002. They moved back to the United States before their first anniversary. Kirk felt he needed more training to understand how to make an impact in Houston, so he and Amanda and their two children spent two years at Wheaton College near Chicago where Kirk got a graduate degree. He spent plenty of time in inner-city Chicago during the weekends working with faith-based community development programs. When he graduated in the summer of 2005, he and Amanda bought a house in Houston. His plan was to start a nonprofit, Agape Development, to provide workforce training programs to inner-city youth. They would partner with an inner-city church to train kids and his dad's dry-cleaning business would hire them.

Shortly after Agape launched, everything changed. As Mike Tyson once said, "Everybody has a plan until they get punched in the face."

Kirk recalls, "Before I started this, I was trying to mitigate the funding and start-up risks. So, I spent a lot of time listening to local leaders. I interviewed several African American pastors and local ministers. What do you see as the real needs, what are the real assets? I read a bunch of books. I did practicums. I was formulating plans. My dad's dry-cleaning business was going to be a way to place youths from my nonprofit into jobs. I knew they could work there and that it was going to be a good fit. I had this local church. I would be under the authority of a pastor there and have his blessing. There was a pipeline with the youth ministry. And I thought, *Man, this is all going to be great.*

"Within twelve months, all of that fell apart. My dad sold his business right when we were launching the ministry. So, I wasn't going to have that automatic in for hires. The church closed. The nonprofit youth ministry merged and moved. And then Labor Day weekend, 2005, Hurricane Katrina hits. Philanthropy in Houston became all about refugee resettlement and helping all of these folks in the Astrodome who were living on cots. Nobody wanted to hear about a job readiness program for young adults.

"By January 2006, most of the things we had in place to mitigate the risk, to ensure we were going to succeed, well, they're all gone. We thought, *Oh my goodness, did we make the biggest mistake of our lives? How are we going to get over this?* Around that time, I was diagnosed with a kidney condition because of my time in Bolivia, and I couldn't get health insurance. I've got two kids, and I don't know how that's going to impact my life. I just thought, *Oh my goodness, this was not the plan. This isn't going to end well.*"

As this turmoil was unfolding, Kirk wrote a business plan for the nonprofit. He started having dessert with his parents' friends and raising money. He finally got to the point where he could establish a first-year budget for the nonprofit of $87,000, with less than half of that going to his compensation. Kirk and Amanda believed it was important to live in the neighborhood that they were serving.

"The neighborhood was really interesting. We lived in a 1,400-square-foot house that we remodeled. If you were to go west and north, the homes started getting big fast. At one end of our block, they got closer to 2,500 square feet. And if you went north to Riverside they got to 3,000, 4,000, 5,000, and 10,000 square feet, so you had some historic wealth.

"However, if you go east and south at the other end, there's an apartment complex where kids are running around. Moms and grandmas doing the best they can to supervise, but the kids were over at our house every day for a popsicle and to jump on the trampoline. You go two blocks south and there's 800-square-foot crack houses. In a quarter of a mile, you can go from a multimillion-dollar home to a crack house and probably 95 percent African American. We stood out as Anglos.

"We now have four children. Our kids' lives were, 'You can't go down in that end, but those kids can come to our house and play.' There was some rough language and rough behavior, and sometimes, we'd have to send kids home. Then you'd go the other direction and we're walking around telling the kids, 'Don't ride your bike on their grass. That's a really nice home.' That dynamic was interesting, but we had way more relationships with the kids from the apartment complex than the families in the big homes.

"We had great neighbors also. We found that every parent wants the same thing for their kids. On our street there were a couple of families that our kids played with the most, they were in charter and magnet schools. Those moms wanted their kids in good schools, to stay safe, to achieve academically. One of those kids, Michael Brown, was on the news last year for being accepted at all the Ivy League schools. Just a brilliant kid—I think he chose Stanford on a full ride. My kids were friends with him and also friends with some kids that were really rough. When they were physical and fought, they had to leave and couldn't come back for a week. Even today, my kids are trying to figure out what sense to make of their childhood and adolescence."

> **LESSON LEARNED:** Gratitude is
> a large proportion of meaning.

Kirk openly admits that he worries about crime and violence. He and his family hear gunshots at night frequently. He and Amanda made sure that his kids didn't go anywhere alone, especially when they were young. Several times, their car has been stolen.

"The other side of this is that even in some of these violent neighborhoods, there are folks living there who are just like you and me. They want a safe neighborhood. They obey the law and wish everybody else did. In our community, that's the majority. But it's the vocal minority that makes the ten o'clock news. It's not as dangerous as it's made out to be in stories that people sell and sensationalize. For the places where the violence is real, I don't want to intentionally put myself in harm's way. I don't go try to bust up gang fights. I don't want to do that. I want to work for the long-term solution."

In the end, Kirk was willing to risk economic opportunity and some degree of safety to make a difference and live out his faith. When he sees the impact on kids growing up in their neighborhood, who become productive citizens, it makes him feel that it's all been worth it. Agape now has a multi-million-dollar annual budget, and some of the youth they trained have come back to take on leadership roles at Agape. Kirk and his family have moved into a different neighborhood, but it's still in an urban, low-income area.

Kirk's whole life is about giving back—to his family, to a community that he loves, and to his faith.

Kirk, Jim Ellis, Gene Gobolys, and Ivo Nelson all committed themselves to giving back, just in very different ways. Kirk dedicated his life to low-income, inner-city youth, consciously choosing to compromise material gains and personal safety. Gene took his uncle's suicide and framed a career around helping struggling entrepreneurs and the planet with clean energy. He and his wife adopted two young brothers from a single-income mom who wanted and needed the help. Jim reconfigured his whole life by marrying a single woman with four kids, then abandoned a successful entrepreneurial career to cultivate the next generation of business leaders at USC. And Ivo realized in the end that giving back, in business and life, is about love.

The common denominator in their stories is using life experiences to understand how best to give back.

We met several others who, like Kirk, Jim, Gene and Ivo, used lessons from life experience to give back. Colter Lewis runs a successful wealth management firm for high-net-worth families in Dallas. When a family member needed his help, Colter didn't hesitate to disrupt his own life and career.

"We've got a tight-knit family, on my wife's side in particular. In 2011, my brother-in-law Jeremy, who I'm very close to, was having severe medical challenges. We eventually found out that his kidneys were failing. This was a guy in his early forties. At the time, I was thirty-nine. Jeremy was on the verge of having to go on dialysis. His two young daughters were close with my daughters, really like surrogate daughters to us."

Colter's blood type was a match. He knew he had to step in and donate a kidney. His young daughters were acutely aware of the risk he was taking.

"I tell my kids a lot about fear, because we live in a world where it's easy to be afraid, especially if you're in high school or junior high—the fear of people laughing at you or the fear of not being successful. I don't want to live a life that's dominated by fear of decisions instead of just doing it. You should let your faith lead you instead of your fear. This was just another opportunity for me to choose that faith over the fear."

Jennifer Stollman is another interviewee who dedicated her life to giving back. She grew up in Michigan, her first four years were spent in foster care before she was adopted by a wealthy family in Bloomfield Hills. She describes her adoptive family as loving but abusive, and her life has been shaped by childhood trauma.

As you would expect from a person coming from this background, Jennifer felt the negative impact of exclusion in her life. Over many years, she transformed that negative energy into positive by facilitating anti-bias training. She spent twenty years in academia, starting with a master's in social justice from Wayne State and then a PhD in history at Michigan. Next came a leadership role at an institute at the University of Mississippi, and now Jennifer has her own anti-bias consulting practice. She has delivered training workshops in some of the toughest, most challenging, and polarized places in the world—including Belfast, South Africa, and even police departments in the American Deep South.

"It's about social justice," she says. "It's equity and inclusion . . . It's also the racism that I've seen. My adopted father and his family were active in the civil rights movement. Somebody's got to do this.

I've pushed things to the limit. For me, I fundamentally believe that inequity can be eliminated.

"I am a religious Jewish person. I believe that our world doesn't have to be as rotten as it's turned out. I do believe that hate is based in fear and anxiety. I can do this. So I'm willing to take the risk every time I step into a session because you do move the needle quite a bit. People change. If you're willing to take that risk, people start to self-reflect. If you make them comfortable and let them know they can move through this, there's incredible satisfaction.

"When I go to bed at night, I don't have to worry about atoning or looking at my life every year. I don't have to worry about that because every day is dedicated to the greater good. And that risk is absolutely worth it. I don't mean to be dramatic, but my life has been under threat, and I'll be okay if it takes me out. There's no better reason to take these types of risks than to make life better for people.

"Also, the thrill is part of the risk . . . When I step into sessions, working in Montgomery, Alabama; Lima, Ohio; Belfast, Ireland, I know that even if I fail abysmally, at least I tried. And chances are I helped at least one person. If you're familiar with the Torah, I really do believe to save one life is to save a nation."

Many Givers find their life mission from the adversity of their own experiences, or from the adversities of their loved ones.

CONCLUSION

We were changed by the risk-taking stories we heard, and we hope you are too.

The Aggregate View

We ended up interviewing one-hundred and two people, fifty-one men and fifty-one women. Most were in their forties or fifties, with enough experience to reflect on their risk-taking choices—and enough time ahead to learn from their mistakes and adjust course. We also talked to seven risk-takers in their thirties who ventured off conventional paths to create their own organizations. The twenty interviews we conducted with those aged sixty-plus revealed the importance of continuing to take risk in the latter stages of life. We found a clear mission and risk-taking orientation is energizing at any age.

Risk-takers are by their nature confident people. Yet there was no one we talked to who made the case they led a perfect life or had it all figured out. Indeed, our interview pool confirms the challenges that all of us face, including those who accomplish much. Fifty-two interviewees revealed a significant life crisis that would have brought many to a grinding halt. Notably, in nearly all cases, rather than becoming emotionally paralyzed, the risk-takers found meaning and understanding of themselves through tumultuous life events. Even when the crisis was the premature death of a loved one.

Eleven interviewees had encountered a significant, life-threatening personal health crisis, in some cases a chronic health condition they continue to live with. They realized that waiting for the perfect time to take a risk can be impractical or even delusional.

Nor did we find the early lives of the risk-takers to be particularly easy. Several were children of immigrants who came to the United States with very little. Twelve grew up poor; sixty-five in the middle-class; and twenty-five grew up wealthy. Those who grew up poor learned the value of money early on, typically working as soon as possible.

Those who grew up rich also experienced significant challenges, just different ones. Often, they faced difficulties around parental expectations that those in the middle class found it easier to escape from. Forty percent of those who grew up wealthy (versus 26 percent overall) mentioned conflict with their parents as a significant challenge in their early lives.

About one-third of interviewees took a huge financial risk along the way—the kind where you don't sleep well for years.

Toward the end of our conversations, we asked interviewees what percentage of their decisions and actions had been driven by nature (genetics) or nurture (their upbringing and life experiences). This has been a longstanding topic in psychology. One researcher framed the debate in these terms:

"The nature versus nurture debate involves the extent to which particular aspects of behavior are a product of either inherited (genetic) or acquired (learned) influences. Nature is what we think of as pre-wiring and is influenced by genetic inheritance and other biological factors. Nurture is generally taken as the influence of external factors after conception, for example, the product of exposure, life experiences, and learning."[17]

Interviewees slightly favored nature (52 percent to 48 percent), although we recorded 100 percent/0 percent nature for some interviewees, 90 percent/10 percent nurture for others, and everything in between.

Risk Livewiths and Risk-Taker Categories

All interviewees demonstrated the six Livewiths, but the degree to which they demonstrated them differed by risk-taker category. To analyze this, we established a dominant risk-taker category for each interviewee and then we scored each interview according to how much the risk-taker demonstrated each Livewith on a scale of one to five.

Livewith One: The Risk Paradox

Even if they didn't articulate it explicitly, risk-takers intuitively understand Livewith One: The Risk Paradox—that the least risky thing you can do with your life is in fact to take risk. Adventurers most strongly demonstrated the Risk Paradox, followed by Idealists.

Vanessa Ogle is primarily an Adventurer and, secondarily, an Idealist.

Vanessa's lived her life embracing the Risk Paradox. She was born in Oklahoma City, but grew up in Dallas/Fort Worth. Her parents divorced when she was young, and she is the oldest of four children. She was always a nerd; she even took a briefcase to junior high.

Vanessa went to college at the University of Texas when she was seventeen and graduated in three years. Vanessa's father was a successful serial entrepreneur, and she self-funded her college education by selling memory chips made by his computer graphics business to the University of Texas.

After college, she joined her father's business, which went through a successful IPO and sale. After the sale, she negotiated to buy the hardware and software part of the business. It took two years, but when the dust settled, Vanessa was CEO of a small business at age twenty-nine.

Vanessa went through over ten years of white-knuckle effort to keep the company afloat, remortgaging her house several times and cutting her salary to $12,000 because it was impossible to get loans from the banks.

"I don't think I was appropriately freaked out," she admits today. "At the time, I didn't understand that I wouldn't be successful. I just knew I had to get it done. I knew I had to succeed. There were so many times in the company's early history where I just couldn't make payroll and then I was barely able to convince a new client to let us design a new product for them."

Finally, she came up with a vision and game plan for generating recurring revenue . . . and it worked.

"In 2017, I announced I'm going to go into this recurring services business and compete with all of my new customers who were buying stuff from us. They were compressing our prices so much, we were having a hard time making money. In our first year we went from having zero hotel properties that we support to fourteen properties. In the second year, we had seventy properties. The third year, we had 280 properties. Today we have 1,900 properties and not just one product, but four that we sell into most of the hotel companies around the world.

"If you've ever watched Netflix on your hotel room TV, that's me. I pioneered being able to get Netflix in a hotel room. I walked into the Netflix offices and convinced the team there to do something they had never done before, which was to allow a technology company to put Netflix on their platform for use in the commercial space."

Today, Vanessa's company supplies the technology that makes TVs in many hotel rooms "smart." The business now has over $75 million in recurring revenue and is growing fast.

Livewith Two: Head and Heart

Survivors were the risk-taker category that rated highest on this Livewith, closely followed by Givers. Both Survivors and Givers understand the importance of heart as they evaluate risk.

We talked to several risk-takers who first figured out how to make enough money to be comfortable, but then realized their heart wasn't in what they were doing professionally.

Kara Festa is a Giver. She grew up in a small town in rural Arizona, and got a civil engineering degree at the University of Arizona in Tucson. She landed at an environmental engineering consulting firm that specialized in wastewater planning and design. Kara spent over twenty years with the firm, eventually making partner, and providing financial support for her stay-at-home-husband and two children.

It was a great professional experience, but Kara had the nagging feeling there must be more to life.

"I had known for several years that I wasn't happy in the organization," she says. "In part, how the direction of the organization was going and my place in it didn't give me any good next steps. So, I'd reached the end of my career potential, and I was pretty aware of that in the last couple of years. And yet, it was hard to let go because it was a very comfortable and lucrative position. It was what I knew, and it was what I'd been doing for twenty years. So, there was a part of me that wanted to let go and there was a part of me that desperately wanted to hang on. There were a couple of years of tug-of-war between those two parts."

On her own initiative, Kara took an integral coaching program to train herself to become a coach. The Moment of Truth came when her father died suddenly in the midst of a chronic health challenge.

"I'd say it was his last gift to me. We talked and reminisced and I realized what he was all about in life. He loved the things he loved with ridiculous passion. He didn't have time for anything that he didn't love. And I knew that about him.

"In those few days after his death, as my siblings and I were talking and reminiscing and consoling each other, I connected with the idea that I needed to go do what I loved. His message to me in those last days was if you don't love it, why are you doing it? It wasn't that he actually said those words to me, but I took that from who he was and how he showed up in the world.

"I went back the next week and gave in my notice. I didn't want to keep hanging on. I wanted to go do something I loved."

Kara decided it was time to listen to her heart. She is now coaching other women, especially those in science and engineering careers, on how to follow their passions.

Livewith Three: Life Is Risk

Not surprisingly, Adventurers most demonstrated this Livewith followed by Survivors, who have viscerally experienced the riskiness of life.

Eileen Brophy is a Survivor. She grew up in the Finger Lakes section of upstate New York, near Syracuse. At nineteen years old, she was pregnant and ended up getting married—but then she was divorced with two children nine years later. Her first husband was abusive. Eileen managed to carve out a successful corporate career as a single mom.

She married her second husband at age thirty-two. It was a good marriage, but her new husband was consumed with work, having started his own industrial janitorial business. When Eileen was thirty-nine, her husband left her a note saying he loved her but couldn't take the pressure any more. He committed suicide.

In the immediate aftermath of the suicide and enormity of her grief, Eileen had to decide what to do with the industrial cleaning business. She wrote a letter the day after her husband died introducing herself to the customers and telling them that she would be keeping the business going.

"Once I made the decision to be invested in this, I had to learn how to do everything because I knew that people would only feel sorry for me for so long," she says. "I had no choice but to learn. I wasn't involved in his business at all, so I didn't know how to use QuickBooks. I wasn't on the bank account, and I couldn't sign checks. I didn't know how to do payroll. I didn't know who the employees were. I didn't even know how to bid a job. I didn't know anything.

"So, I literally worked from six in the morning until midnight every day for weeks and months. The months turned into years. Thank God I had some amazing clients that were amazing friends. I said to one of them, 'I don't know how to bid a job.' He said, 'You take your wage times this times that, and there's your cost.' Well, how do I clean? What do we clean? What do we use? And how do you tell people this is what you do? If somebody calls and wants to ask you to clean their facility, how do you know what to do?"

Eileen took advantage of every possible opportunity to learn how to run a business. Twelve years later, the business has grown more than three-fold, and she has remarried.

Livewith Four: Risk Never Fails to Teach

Liberators were rated highest on the fourth Livewith. The Liberators that we met didn't spend much time introspecting on setbacks or failures. They were too busy moving on with their lives.

Many Liberators are driven by an intense curiosity to learn.

Ana Sanchez grew up in Madrid, the daughter of a successful tech entrepreneur. Ana was always shy, but in every major step of her life she's found a way to take risks and learn from them. She attributes this to her curiosity and desire to learn: "My curiosity has always been so big that that has trumped my discomfort. I'm curious to the point that I'm curious about how I'll react to being that uncomfortable."

Ana took her first major risk in high school, when she asked her parents if she could spend her senior year in the United States. Her parents' relationship was dysfunctional and they eventually divorced. Ana wanted to spend some time away from Madrid, and her parents agreed to put her into an exchange program, so she spent that year at Put-in-Bay, Ohio, attending high school on a remote island in the middle of Lake Erie. There were only three seniors in Ana's graduating class.

After spending her late teens and early twenties in Spain and Germany, Ana took her second major risk when she agreed to move to Florida to run the US office of her father's software company. When her father shut down the office a year later, Ana decided to stay and got a degree from the Art Institute in Fort Lauderdale. She met her future husband, who is from Israel, in Florida, and together they have created a successful custom digital design company, which they started by taking out credit card debt. It took three years for them to get out of debt; when they finally had some money in the bank Ana felt that they were wealthy. Ten years and one daughter later, they haven't looked back.

Ana has pushed through her shyness to move to the United States, and become a US citizen and successful entrepreneur. She turned down several corporate jobs along the way in order to create her own life. Every major step that Ana has taken with her life has been about learning.

Livewith Five: Risk Tastes Different with Age

Seekers most strongly exhibited this Livewith, perhaps because it is in the nature of seeking to keep experimenting with options— and, once you accomplish something, to look forward for the next challenge.

Michele Morris is a Seeker who is working on her third distinctly different career.

Michele met her future husband, Greg, when she was eighteen, married seven years later, and had three kids by the time she was thirty. By then, she was also a successful IBM executive living in Denver. But when her oldest son starting having problems in high school, Michele decided she had to leave IBM mid-career because she couldn't help her son and travel around the world on business simultaneously.

"I had just achieved this executive role within IBM," she says. "And about that time, my son was maybe fifteen or sixteen. He had been struggling in school. He had been diagnosed with Type 1 diabetes and started rebelling. He started smoking weed and drinking and doing everything he shouldn't be doing. At one point, I was presenting my strategy to the division executive, one of the top twenty people in IBM. I was interrupted by my secretary to tell me the police were on the phone and I needed to leave the meeting. That caused me to question what I was doing pursuing this executive career."

Michele always had a passion for food. After leaving IBM, she started a catering business in Denver. It took several years to make it work, but when it did, she found gratification and meaning that she never achieved at IBM.

"I started out saying, 'I'm only going to do private and small group cooking classes and cooking dinner parties. I'm not going to cater.' Sure enough, somewhere along the line, people asked me to cater. Catering led to some different food opportunities, such as that first recipe column where I only got paid twenty-five dollars. I'm sure I spent more than that in purchasing the food to write it. But by doing that, I established myself as a food writer. That led to more opportunities. I met somebody in the Colorado Author's League who was presented a cookbook contract opportunity that she couldn't handle. She respected my work, and she referred the publisher to me. That first cookbook won the Colorado Book Award, and the publisher let me use my own food photography. All of a sudden, I've established myself as a food photographer. The food photography led to opportunities to do recipe development and food photography for some big-name clients like Niman Ranch's beef and Prairie Grove Farms' pork."

Michele's new career grew with her reputation in the food community. However, when she was in her mid-fifties, her husband got sick suddenly while they were in Europe on vacation.

"My husband collapsed when we landed in the Madrid airport in October 2016. He had a ruptured brain aneurysm. Unbelievably, he lived for six months and died in April 2017. Right after his death, I went back to teaching and catering and food writing. Then I wrote a memoir about that experience originally for my own therapy. And then, through a personal connection, I ended up joining a foundation that supports families impacted by brain aneurysms."

Today, Michele is actively involved in raising money for that foundation and is re-inventing herself once more.

Livewith Six: Mission Transforms Risk

We saw again and again in our interviews how a strong sense of mission overcomes the hesitation to take risk—especially when it comes to Idealists, the risk-takers who are most dominantly driven by mission, with Givers being a close second.

Yildiz Blackstone grew up in Izmir, Turkey. Her parents owned a successful department store, but Yildiz always viewed America as the land of opportunity and wanted to make it on her own in the fashion industry. When she was twenty and had graduated from college in Turkey, her parents let her spend a year in California. She wanted to go to the Fashion Institute of Technology in New York City, but the year before they had rejected her application.

While visiting New York City on Christmas break, Yildiz stopped by the Fashion Institute on a Sunday five minutes before the office closed.

"I asked my friend to stop the car, and I went straight into the school," she says. "It was Christmas break and they were closing. I marched into the administrator's office and I asked her, 'Why did you not accept me?' She asked, 'Who are you?' I said, 'I'm Yildiz from Izmir, Turkey. I applied last year and I got a refusal.'

"It was Sunday. There were no computers. She opened my file; she found it within seconds. She said, 'Why would we accept you? You are a D or F student.' I said, 'What are you talking about?' She said, 'You are 64 out of 100 GPA on average.' I said, "No, 50 is the passing grade and no one gets over 65 in our school system, because they don't give grades. Give me another chance.'

"I applied again and they accepted me that time."

Yildiz had a hard time finding a job in New York after graduating. Finally, on the day she was supposed to leave for Turkey, she got a call, went on an interview, and landed an entry-level job. She had to call her mom and explain she wouldn't be returning home.

After getting fired from two jobs, mostly for speaking her mind, Yildiz worked a retail sales job for Versace, helping with the opening of their first retail store in New York. It was the high days of Versace, and she was in her element.

Then came Yildiz's big break.

"I met a young Italian man named Luca Orlandi. I was twenty-three years old by then, and he was two years older. He had a dream. He wanted to start a fashion company. I had a secure job at Versace, and it was the brand that I loved. I did my thesis on Versace. Gianni Versace, at the time, used to come to the store. He was like a movie star. It was a dream job for me.

"Anyway, Luca wanted someone to build his brand while he designed it. I just jumped on it because I knew this was my chance to make it on my own. It was going to be an adventure, an unknown, and I would be the sole person to make it or break it in terms of business. It was so natural. And to me, it was an immediate yes.

"It was a start-up, really. Just him and me at first. I opened the first store, and the rest is history. We built the company, Luca Luca, over twenty years. It was a difficult journey because building a brand in the sea of established designers, monopolies, and huge financial competitors, we were nobody. We were two youngsters with a dream. Luca's dream was to be this fashion hub for the youth of today. It sounded awesome to me. Everything was a fight to get the location in Bal Harbour Shops or in Houston Galleria, or get a great time slot in fashion week. Each phase was a huge stress and huge fight, and I loved it."

Eventually, Luca Luca was sold to a private equity firm. And Yildiz went on a blind date, met her future husband who was a music industry executive, got married in New York, and became a US citizen. But Yildiz had found her passion for the fashion industry. Today, she and her sister have created and act as brand ambassadors for a successful fashion events business, which connects creative design talent to wealthy women who desire cutting-edge couture.

The Female View of Risk

We didn't begin our project looking for gender differences in viewing risk, but female interviewees began to proactively mention them. So, we began asking them if they thought there were such differences, and most said they thought there were.

It was our interview with Sandi Webster that first suggested this was a topic worth exploring.

Sandi was born in Jamaica but immigrated to Brooklyn when she was three years old. Her mother worked multiple jobs, and they grew up poor. Sandi was an entrepreneur from her teenage years, and it took her many years of work and school to get through college. When she was young, she discovered she could make money (a dollar per house) turning the lights on and off for the Jewish families in her neighborhood when they were observing Sabbath.

Sandi eventually landed at American Express, where she developed an expertise in marketing analytics. After 9/11, when she was forty years old, she was laid off. She then formed a marketing consulting firm, exclusively employing women who wanted more flexible work arrangements than their corporate employers would allow. Sandi and her business partner successfully grew the business and sold it to a private equity firm in 2016.

During the course of Sandi's busy and eventful life, she raised two adoptive children. When we asked her about gender differences in evaluating risk, she had a clear viewpoint:

"Well, I think boys are raised differently. You can't minimize that in how their risk assessment happens. Starting from a number's perspective, almost automatically, boys are thought to be better at math than girls. You see that in schools—you steer the girls to the language and communication and marketing track, and you steer the boys to the engineering and science track.

"This is what all the STEM programs are about. It's how you relate the mindset of someone at an earlier age. So, boys are told they're better with numbers, although I knew I could 'outnumber' a lot of guys. But they were told, so they developed the confidence and the belief that they're better at this. And risk is really about numbers. It's thinking in bets. That's what decision-making is.

"So, guys were taught to take chances. I think that's probably the best way I can say it. Girls were taught not to take chances. By steering them to particular careers, it gives rationalization to how women think of risk.

"Girls are taught that even if your man goes to work, you are really the center and head of the family. So, whatever money he makes, you have to figure out how to use it. If you only make ten dollars a week, you have to figure out how to make that ten dollars work for your family. But the world looks at it as not what the woman is doing with the money, but how the man is making the money. If you ask, who's the head of household, it's going to be the man because he's the one making the money.

"When a woman sits down and thinks about life, it's often about family security. That's at the top of our mind—my family and my financial security. The man also has an idea that his kids are going to be taken care of. That woman is still going to take care of his kids even if he walks away. They don't have the same emotional risk at stake."

Of course, efforts to understand gender differences risk over-generalization. However, most of those who thought there were gender differences spoke eloquently of the high degree to which women factored family considerations into whatever risk they were considering. And many female risk-takers, such as Jennifer Maanavi, turned the inflexibility of their corporate employers when it came to supporting working mothers into their launching pad for going out on their own.

Elizabeth Miller didn't emphasize her gender when we interviewed her, but it quickly became clear that her career was deeply influenced by how others in financial services perceived women with careers in the 1980s and 1990s. After graduating from the University of Pennsylvania, Elizabeth went to work on Wall Street in a trading group. "There weren't a whole lot of women mentors and leaders on Wall Street at the time," she says. "I didn't have any negative experiences, but neither were there clear paths to follow."

Elizabeth took a positive view of her experiences. "The great thing about a career for women in financial services is that the numbers don't lie. If you have a great performance record, your gender doesn't really matter. You've proven that you're worthy."

When Elizabeth was in her early forties, she was at a wealth management firm focused on multi-generational family wealth and the male founders began to retire. Elizabeth soon realized that she had run straight into a gender issue. "That was the first time in my career where I reached a point where I thought I was being held back simply because I was a woman. I'd always been treated well by the partners. But one partner just didn't see a woman as the CEO of a firm he had helped grow."

Elizabeth decided to create her own wealth management firm. Her husband was incredibly supportive; a huge believer that she could do it. It was the fall of 2008, just as Lehman Brothers collapsed and the market meltdown was in full force. She called her husband at work, and "he gave me the courage to say, okay, we're going to do this."

Today, Elizabeth runs her own small and successful wealth management firm in northern New Jersey. Over time, she's come to realize how much even her teenage daughters learned from her taking the risk to start her own firm. "I hear them talking with friends. They are very proud of the business I created. They're very proud of what I do. I mean, wow, how many parents can say that? I just think had I known taking that risk and starting that business was going to teach them how to watch something germinate and grow and have some ups and downs, but be proud of building something, yeah, I think I would've taken that step even more aggressively."

We wondered how women earlier in their career view risk-taking. Then we met Lauren Reed. Lauren grew up in St. Louis. Her father was an entrepreneur, but money was always a concern for the family. Lauren realized at a young age the need to be financially independent.

After studying marketing and communications in college, Lauren went to work for an ad agency. After eight years, the agency imploded. They had grown too fast, and there was conflict between the managing partners. Lauren left and began to do freelance work, but one of her key clients from the ad agency reached out to her. Based on that conversation, Lauren decided to create a digital agency of her own.

Lauren is a Liberator: she values her independence, and she hasn't had good experiences working in other cultures. "After my experience at my last agency and what I learned, I realized I didn't want my destiny in anyone else's hands. Running my own agency, I have twenty clients I work with on a day-to-day basis who can fire me. If I go work for someone else, there's one person who can decide to fire me."

Lauren has now run her own agency in Nashville for over seven years. Within a few weeks of starting the agency, she had about

$250,000 in annual billings. Every year since, the agency has grown at least 10 percent, including the two years when she had her children. She has several major corporate clients and eleven full-time employees.

Lauren focuses deeply on creating the right kind of culture:

"I went through a quarter-life crisis a few years ago where I thought, *All I've ever done is work in an agency, and it's all I'm going to do. I'm thirty-seven.* But then it hit me. What I'm doing now and what I'm providing is a really great workplace culture. My filters on my agency decisions are, am I providing a workplace I'd want my children, particularly my daughter, to work at?

"So, we make a lot of decisions from the cultural perspective. We provide full maternity coverage. A company of my size is not required to do that and it's hard, but we do. We provide full benefits. Again, a company the size of mine is not required to give that, but it's just really important to me; I feel a duty to provide a great workplace for women. It is not by design, but we are all women right now. I'm the oldest. Our employees range from twenty-five to thirty-five years old. A lot of them are getting engaged, getting married, having their first babies, that sort of thing. I just want to show them it can be done. You can have a great life and a great career, and it's not one or the other."

Lauren wants the business to support her lifestyle and her family—not drive her life. In the past few years, she's taken three to four weeks off several times to travel. Mostly what she's learned is that the business can survive without her, which has freed her up to focus on more strategic issues. When an employee suggested that they form a foundation, Lauren loved the idea. In the past few years, they've funded more than fifty people to do volunteer work in poverty-stricken countries overseas.

When we asked Lauren if she thought there were differences between how men and women made decisions, she didn't hesitate. "I make decisions with my heart. I don't know if that's gender-based or it's just me. But sometimes, the data doesn't add up for me, and I'm going to go forward with the decision anyway. So, I follow my gut and my heart a lot. I don't know that men follow their heart as much when making decisions."

After hearing that, we looked at our data for Livewith Two: Head and Heart. When we scored each interviewee for the degree to which they demonstrated the Livewiths on a scale of 1 to 5, men averaged 3.5 in demonstrating this Livewith, whereas women averaged quite a bit higher, nearly 4.0. We understand our sample size is relatively small; having said that, more women than men explicitly mentioned the importance of listening to their heart in making risk-taking decisions.

When we analyzed our aggregate survey data for other gender differences, we found two that were noteworthy:

- Risk-taker Categories—Of the seven Adventurers, six were men and one was a woman. Nearly 40 percent of women interviewees were Liberators, and only 27 percent of men. Corporate life did not accommodate these women's work-life balance, motivating them to strike out on their own.

- Nature/Nurture—In response to our nature/nurture question, on average, women responded 50/50 and men responded 60/40. We are not developmental psychologists, but anecdotally it seems that more men are told early in life that they are wired for professional success.

Risk and Aging

We were curious how risk is perceived differently as people age. Researchers have found that brain chemistry changes as people age, with the fast, instinctive thinking style of youth giving way to a more holistic fast and slow thinking.

Our interviewees convinced us that continuing to take risks is important as we age or, as one put it succinctly, "Life is risk." When we interviewed Michael Saltman, now in his seventies, his last comment was that he was "not letting the old man in." Indeed, this may very well be the healthiest way to live.

We also noticed that the nature of risk-taking often changes as one ages. Many risk-takers took huge financial risks when they were younger, often feeling that they had little to lose. As they achieve financial security, some (but not all) become more financially risk-averse due to family obligations. And for those who have achieved financial success, it becomes less important over time.

As we age, our physical sense of taste changes—we still need to eat, but the food and drink that we savor changes. The same is true of our perceptions of risk. As we age, many are more willing to risk self-perceptions and relationship to gain something important. Peter Denning had all the money one could possibly need but risked his relationship with his father to break free and live his own life. For Alton Butler, resurrecting his relationship with his father was an essential risk to take after he had "made it" professionally.

Risk Is Personal—
But You Can Learn from Others

We began this project with common interests. Why do people take big risks, and how do they work out? Can we identify patterns of successful risk-takers? If so, what are those patterns? What causes people to make disruptive changes in their life? And, by extension, why do some people avoid risk-taking at all costs?

We were particularly interested in risk-taking that is viewed as inadvisable in conventional circles. Alan took exactly such a risk when he abandoned his medical residency in his late twenties to start a software company. Doug dabbled in risk-taking but usually within the confines of a large corporate structure.

Yet we shared an insatiable curiosity about what motivates risk-takers. And we believed, at a minimum, we would meet some fascinating people along the journey. In this, we were certainly not disappointed.

We learned emphatically that there is no monolithic description of a risk-taker. They come in all human configurations, and they are driven by many motivations. Not all risk-takers are introspective by nature. The vast majority of our interviewees welcomed the chance to reflect back on their own journeys because it was the first time they had ever paused to do so.

Risk-takers have multiple motivations, but we found it possible to categorize them. Adventurers are driven by the thrill that comes with risk-taking. Liberators create their own independence. Idealists follow a sense of mission. Survivors transcend their tumultuous or traumatic circumstances. Seekers risk to understand themselves. Givers are inspired by giving back to the world.

In the end, risk-taking is an intensely personal journey. When the great mythologist Joseph Campbell implored us to "follow your bliss," he didn't really intend us to live a hedonistic existence. He meant that we each need to find our own path, and that no one else can find it for us.

While each of us must find our own path, the good news—and

we think it is good news, indeed—is that we can learn from the life stories of others. Perhaps we can find in others' lives the courage and inspiration to motivate us to act—to keep taking our own risks. We learned how taking those risks often leads to unanticipated new paths in life.

No matter where we are in our journey through life, we can still seek to understand ourselves better. We can ask ourselves what motivates us to take risk. What risk-taker category are we now, at this stage of life? We can ask how our own lives demonstrate the Risk Paradox, that the least risky thing we can do with our life is to take risks. We can understand the degree to which the Livewiths play out in our own lives. Most importantly, we can use the stories in this book to become the best possible versions of ourselves.

We wrote this book to help you ask these questions of your own life. Thank you for going on this journey with us. If even one of you has been motivated by these stories to make positive changes, to take that next step in your journey, to take more risk—we are deeply grateful.

And the world is already a better place for your having done so.

APPENDIX A

Key Risk Concepts

Burning the Boats: The tendency of risk-takers to eliminate the option of going backward to earlier choices, so that they are all-in on the risk they are taking.

Financial Maximization: Making life and career decisions with the overriding goal of maximizing wealth and consumption.

Flow State: Flow state tends to occur when a person's skills are fully involved in overcoming a challenge that is just about manageable. Optimal experiences usually involve a fine balance between one's ability to act and the available opportunities for action. If the challenges are too high, one gets frustrated, then worried, and eventually anxious. If the challenges are too low relative to one's skills, one gets relaxed, then bored. But when high challenges are matched with high skills, then the deep involvement that sets flow apart from ordinary life is likely to occur.

Inner Fulfillment Risk: When people have everything they need, materially, they often experience emptiness. And they often need to take more risks for inner fulfillment.

Life Fulfillment Maximization: Life fulfillment maximization is distinctly different than financial maximization. You live a fulfilling life by marrying what you are good at with what you love to do.

Loss Aversion Bias: When the decision to take a risk is driven more by loss aversion than gain. In other words, by the comparison of what could be lost by taking the risk, compared to what could be lost by *not* taking the risk.[18]

Moments of Truth: All of us face Moments of Truth in our lives: forks in the road where we must decide whether or not to choose risk or more near-term certainty. The riskier choice always involves potential downsides—that's basically what risk means. It's not like we need to take the riskier fork in the road at every turn, but if we never choose risk and adventure, we can easily end up with a life full of regrets for paths not chosen.

Risk Avoidance Fallacy: Believing that you can avoid risk by staying in your current situation because it will not change. Everything changes.

Risk Driver: The motivations to take a risk. In this book, we've explored Experience Seeking, Independence, Changing the World, Life Survival, Finding Yourself, and Serving Others.

Risk Orientation: An individual's personal viewpoint or conceptualization of risk-taking.

Right Time Fallacy: The notion, unsupported by our work, that the risk-taker will or should wait for "the right time" in their life to take a risk that leads to a successful outcome.

Risk Heuristic: An approach to risk-taking that employs a practical method, not guaranteed to be optimal, perfect, logical, or rational, but instead sufficient for reaching an immediate goal. Heuristics are mental shortcuts.

Self-Esteem Risk: When what is being risked is primarily one's self-esteem.

Smart Risk: Any risk that is taken with consideration to both rational and emotional needs, as well as the upside and the downside of taking the risk and not taking the risk—independent of the outcome.

The Risk Paradox: The notion that taking a risk is the least risky thing that you can do, in order to live a fulfilling life.

Risk-Taker Interview Results

Risk-Taker Interviews Summary Results

Demographics

Men 51, **Women** 51

Age Range

30–39	7
40–49	45
50–59	28
60–69	14
70–79	5
80–89	1

Life Characteristics

Significant Life Crisis? **Yes** 52, **No** 50

Significant Personal Health Crisis? **Yes** 11, **No** 91

Grew Up

Poor	12
Middle Class	66
Rich	24

Had Teenage Business? **Yes** 19, **No** 83

Took Huge Financial Risk? **Yes** 34, **No** 68

Been Divorced? **Yes** 25, **No** 77

Parental Conflict? **Yes** 24, **No** 78

Siblings? **Yes** 85, **No** 17

Children? **Yes** 85, **No** 17

Risk-Takers by Motivating Category

Adventurers	7
Liberators	32
Survivors	16
Idealists	20
Givers	12
Seekers	15

Do you believe your actions and decisions are more driven by nature or nurture? Please provide a specific percentage

Average for Nature	52.66%
Average for Nurture	47.34%

Strength of Risk Livewiths by Risk-Taker Category

Risk-Taker Category	1. Risk Paradox	2. Head and Heart	3. All Life *Is* Risky	4. Risk Never Fails to Teach	5. Risk Tastes Different with Age	6. Mission Trans-forms Risk
Adventurers	*Very High*	*High*	*Very High*	*High*	*High*	*Medium*
Liberators	*High*	*High*	*High*	*High*	*Medium*	*Medium*
Idealists	*Very High*	*High*	*High*	*Medium*	*High*	*Very High*
Survivors	*High*	*Very High*	*High*	*Medium*	*High*	*High*
Seekers	*High*	*Very High*	*High*	*High*	*High*	*High*
Givers	*High*	*High*	*High*	*Medium*	*High*	*Very High*

APPENDIX C

Subject Citation Index

ACKNOWLEDGMENTS

Doug Schneider

Writing any book is no small undertaking, as anyone who has ever done it knows. This book would have never been completed without the incredible work of my co-author, Alan, who seems to relish large challenges. Alan conducted all of the interviews, and he contributed greatly to the structure of this book. I am deeply grateful to the 102 fascinating people who agreed to be interviewed, and whose own life stories inspire me to keep working on mine. I am also very thankful for the work of our editor, Bryony Sutherland. This is my second book working with Bryony, and I marvel at her professionalism, competence, and ability to turn my writing into an actual book.

My own life is immensely blessed by my marriage to my wife, Elaine, who always encourages me to take on every risk, however inadvisable—and then stands with me. There is not a word that I have ever published anywhere that I have not read out loud to her first.

Alan Ying

Everyone has a book in them. After getting here, I can now share the secret to writing a book: become really good friends with an author whose style you admire, then engage in a years-long campaign to make them want to write a book with you. Thanks, Doug. From the moment we met I knew we'd be friends for a long time.

This was a worldwide effort mostly by people who didn't know me. To the hundreds who referred me to interviewee candidates: thank you for bringing the stories of these incredible people to the world.

To the interviewees: the hundreds of hours I spent talking with you inspired and humbled me. I laughed, I cried, I exclaimed with surprise and delight, and I sweated breathlessly as you shared your intimate life experiences. All of you agreed to share your story in the hopes that your lessons learned might inspire, educate, help, or otherwise touch just one person. It was our greatest motivation to honor your efforts. Thank you.

To my family: I conducted the interviews talking at jet engine volume, clomping around the house, and gesticulating as if swatting bees around my head. For a year. My lovely wife, Anita; my children, Sydney, Emory, and Cooper; and my father, Chen, all tolerated this without complaint. I'm more fortunate than I deserve.

ENDNOTES

1   Kayt Sukel, *The Art of Risk: The Ne w Science of Courage, Caution, & Chance* (Washington, DC: National Geographic Society, 2016), 51.

2   Michael Lewis, *The Undoing Project: A Friendship That Changed Our Minds* (W. W. Norton and Company: New York, 2016).

3   Doug Sundheim, *Taking Smart Risks: How Sharp Leaders Win When Stakes Are High*, (New York: McGraw-Hill Education, 2013), 19–20.

4   Sukel, 56.

5   Malcolm Gladwell, *The Tipping Point: How Little Things Can Make a Big Difference* (New York: Little, Brown, and Company, 2000).

6   Sukel, 119–120.

7   Dayton Duncan and Ken Burns, *Lewis & Clark: The Journey of the Corps of Discovery: An Illustrated History* (Knopf: New York, 1999), 160–161.

8   Duncan and Burns, 207.

9   Mihaly Csikszentmihalyi, *Finding Flow: The Psychology of Engagement with Everyday Life*, (New York: Basic Books, 1997), 30-31.

10   Daniel H. Pink, *Free Agent Nation: How America's New Independent Workers Are Transforming the Way We Live* (New York: Warner Books, 2001).

11   Pink, 55.

12   Pink, 48.

13   Irin Carmon and Shana Knizhnik, *Notorious RBG: The Life and Times of Ruth Bader Ginsburg* (New York: Dey Street Books, 2015).

14   Marc J. Seifer, *Wizard: The Life and Times of Nikola Tesla: Biography of a Genius* (New York: Citadel Press, 2016), 98.

15   Seifer, *Wizard: The Life and Times of Nikola Tesla*.

16   Nell Irvin Painter, *Sojourner Truth: A Life, A Symbol* (New York: W. W. Norton & Company, 1997), 113.

17   Saul McCleod, SimplyPyschology.org, updated 2018, https://www.simply psychology.org/naturevsnurture.html.

18   Michael Lewis, *The Undoing Project: A Friendship That Changed Our Minds* (W. W. Norton and Company: New York, 2016).

ABOUT THE AUTHORS

Alan Ying dropped out of the cardiothoracic surgery residency program at Duke University to start a software company when he was twenty-eight years old. Since selling that business, he's enjoyed leading, investing in, and serving on the boards of start-ups to public companies. Alan grew up in Ohio and now lives in Texas. He is married to Anita and is father to Sydney, Emory, and Cooper (hey kids, your names are in a book!). You can email him at alan.j.ying@gmail.com.

Doug Schneider spent over twenty-five years in high-tech firms, many of them leading and working in healthcare information technology firms that drove industry expansion. He's had a lifelong focus on innovation and risk-taking. Doug is also the author of the running memoir, *Ten Marathons: Searching for the Soft Ground in a Hard World*. He splits his time between Cincinnati, Ohio and Hilton Head, South Carolina with his wife, Elaine. Doug's writing on life, work, and running can be found at www.dougschneider.net and he can also be reached by email at marathondoug@hotmail.com.